Mountain Biking
the Appalachians

Northwest
North Carolina

Southwest
Virginia

ALSO BY LORI FINLEY

Mountain Biking the Appalachians: Brevard-Asheville/The Pisgah Forest
Mountain Biking the Appalachians: Highlands-Cashiers
The Mountain Biker's Guide to the Southeast (Menasha Ridge Press)

MOUNTAIN BIKING
THE APPALACHIANS

Northwest North Carolina
Southwest Virginia

Lori Finley

John F. Blair, Publisher
Winston-Salem, North Carolina

BOOK DESIGN BY DEBRA LONG HAMPTON

MAPS BY THE ROBERTS GROUP

COVER PHOTOGRAPH BY DENNIS COELLO

PRINTED AND BOUND BY R. R. DONNELLEY & SONS

Library of Congress Cataloging-In-Publication Data

Finley, Lori, 1958–
    Mountain biking the Appalachians.   Northwest North
Carolina / southwest Virginia / by Lori Finley.
        p.   cm.
    Includes index.
    ISBN 0-89587-114-9
    1. All terrain cycling—North Carolina—Guidebooks.   2. All
terrain cycling—Virginia—Guidebooks.   3. North Carolina—Guidebooks.
4. Virginia—Guidebooks.   I. Title.
GV1045.5.N75F56   1994
796.6'4'09756—dc20   94–20982

For Fred and Sandra

Locator Map for Trail Rides

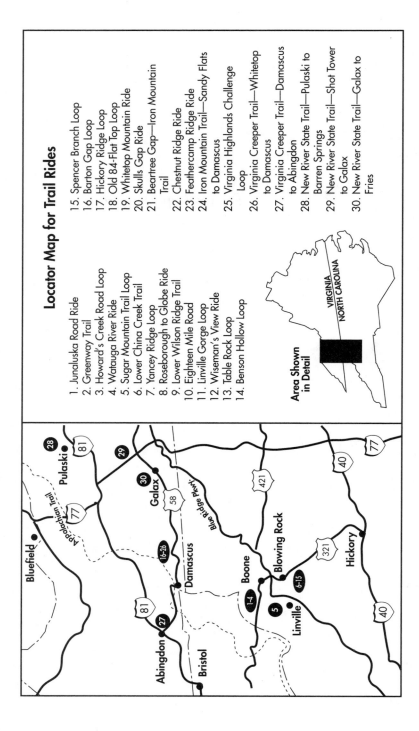

Contents

Rail Trails

Acknowledgments

Many people helped me in the research and riding required for this book, and to them all I offer a hearty word of thanks.

First, I would like to thank Sarah and Mike Boone, owners of Magic Cycles in Boone, North Carolina. They eagerly told me about the area's classic mountain-bike rides and then spent quite a bit of time guiding me on the trails. I had a great time getting to know both of these good people while pedaling through the forests, and I appreciate everything they did to help me.

I also want to thank the staff of Rock & Roll Sports in Boone, who spent a considerable chunk of time in the back of the store tracing rides on maps. A few of the customers in the store, including John Holder, even took the time to tell me about a favorite ride or two. The staff of Blue Planet Maps, including Mark Stroud, was quite helpful when I began the research for this book and always quickly mailed topographical maps to me when I needed them.

A word of thanks is also due Byrum Geisler, Kim Schmidinger, the staff of the Map Shop in Greenville, South Carolina, and Dennis Barnes of Denny's Stop & Go in Barren Springs, Virginia.

A special word of thanks goes to Jo Jo and Woody Keen of Blowing Rock, North Carolina, for literally going the extra mile to help me. I want to thank them for the hours spent trail riding, for the miles of dirt roads driven, and for their open-door hospitality. I have never transcribed trail notes in a prettier setting than the deck of their beautiful mountain home. I'm spoiled now. How can I possibly write in the future without a view of Grandfather Mountain and without hearing the song of their wind chimes? I especially want to thank Woody for the bike repairs, for keeping good tunes crooning from the stereo, and for keeping the cats preoccupied while Jo Jo and I sprawled out on the den rug for late-night map study sessions.

Countless federal, state, and county employees helped me obtain accurate trail information. These people were always friendly, helpful, and brimming with quick answers to my questions. I particularly want to thank Phil Kromer of Pisgah National Forest's Grandfather District. A good friend to the High Country Mountain Bike Association, Phil took the time to answer all of my questions and to provide me with accurate information on trails in his district. I also want to thank Judy Johnson at New River Trail State Park for the mad faxing and for all her help.

Thanks to Angie and Roy Costner for taking care of my sweet daughters on the many occasions when my friends and I drove off at the crack of dawn in cars laden with mountain bikes.

And to my friends who have been with me on the trails for years now, I offer my heartfelt thanks. Sandra Thomas, Fred Thomas, Jim Sinclair, Brenda Cox, Herb Clark, and Owen Riley have stuck with me during the good times as well as the occasional bad. Despite enduring shuttle rides from hell, riding tortuous exploratory loops that took us to points unknown, and flirting with dusk because I wanted to check out one more "quick" ride, these good friends always rejoined me on the trails whenever I asked. Thanks for the help and the good memories. Years from now, these times will be my "good old days."

I especially want to thank the staff at John F. Blair, Publisher, for not being too upset when an ill-timed knee fracture took me off the trails and threw the book's production behind schedule. Thanks to all of you for working so hard under pressure to make this book what it is.

And finally, a special word of thanks goes to my family—Bob, Erin, and Elizabeth—for their support, encouragement, and pride. I couldn't have done it without you.

Introduction

Imagine the sounds of a mountain creek singing off in the distance, the call of a red-tailed hawk, and the rustle of dry leaves skittering across a narrow trail. Think of the warm smell of a grassy meadow, the sweet fragrance of mountain magnolia blossoms, and the scent of high-elevation fir trees, calling up memories of Christmas morning. Picture a sun-drenched dirt road, a springtime hardwood forest exploding into a thousand shades of green, and a snow-encrusted mountain bald sparkling under a clear winter sky.

When you have summoned all of these to mind, you will have imagined the setting for some of the finest riding in the country. Welcome to mountain biking in the Appalachians.

The high country of northwest North Carolina and southwest Virginia is laced with a labyrinth of single-track trails, logging roads, and overgrown jeep tracks that beckon mountain bikers. For every route pedaled, there are a dozen more within a stone's throw, just waiting to be discovered. In fact, there are enough miles of designated trails and dirt roads that a cyclist could quit his job and easily spend a year or so exploring. But for the weekend warrior who doesn't have the luxury of full-time exploration, this guide features some of the classic rides of the region.

The 30 rides covered here will appeal to cyclists of diverse ability, experience, and even mood. Some trails hug the banks of low-lying rivers, while others climb into deep, hidden pockets of dense forest high in the hills. Ridden as loops, out-and-backs, and one-way shuttle rides, they range in difficulty from easy to strenuous, and in length from about 4 miles to about 50 miles.

With all these rides have to offer, you would expect to find crowds galore and wall-to-wall Lycra and titanium on any given weekend. But for whatever reason, these trails and roads have remained virtually undiscovered.

Pick up any mountain-bike magazine and you are sure to find its pages splattered with places like Moab and Crested

Butte. Even North Carolina's Tsali trails have been featured. But have you read about the lofty Mount Rogers area in Virginia? How about the New River Trail? Have you even heard of North Carolina's Wilson Creek? Probably not, though outstanding mountain-biking opportunities abound in these areas.

"If the nearest town to Wilson Creek was San Francisco instead of Linville and Blowing Rock, its trails would be as known nationally as those in Marin," writes Dennis Coello in a *Bike* magazine article featuring unacclaimed cycling haunts. It's true. It's also true that many of these sites are relatively young. For example, the Mount Rogers area was established in the mid-1960s. And the rail trails described are part of a recent movement to convert abandoned railway corridors into multiuse recreation areas.

Though these spots are virtually crowd-free for now, enjoy the solitude while you can. Mountain biking this good will not remain untouched by fame for long.

Planning a Trip

Location

Half the mountain-bike rides in this guidebook are located in northwest North Carolina, near the towns of Boone and Blowing Rock. The other half are located in southwest Virginia, the majority in Mount Rogers National Recreation Area.

Routes

The routes described in this guidebook are grouped according to their location. Most can be completed in a day, many in half a day. Longer rides, such as the Linville Gorge Loop and the Virginia Creeper Trail, can be split up into several days by making lodging arrangements at points along the way in advance.

Before You Go

Before riding, it is advisable to check with the appropriate land administrators—the United States Forest Service, state parks, city parks, etc.—to confirm that the ride is open for mountain-bike use. At the time of this writing, all the routes covered were open to mountain bikers. But as we all know, a cloud of land-use controversy hangs over many mountain-biking areas. Land status is in a constant state of flux, and designations do change. *You* are ultimately responsible for ensuring that a trail is legal for pedaling. If you arrive at a trailhead and find that a No Mountain Biking sign has been posted, heed it. There are always plenty of other rides nearby.

Seasons

Because of the relatively mild winters in northwest North Carolina and southwest Virginia, most of these trails can be ridden year-round. Occasionally, they will be covered by snow or ice, particularly at the higher elevations. Some trails require river or creek crossings and should be avoided during cold weather, due to the risk of hypothermia. There are also some trails that should be avoided after periods of heavy rain, because of muddy conditions. These special considerations are noted in the individual ride descriptions. Mountain showers can be expected almost every day during the summer and are often a welcome, cooling relief from the heat. Hunting is permitted in some of the areas covered; mountain bikers are advised to wear fluorescent orange or some other bright, unnatural color.

Equipment and Essentials

Bicycle

A mountain bike with fat, knobby tires is necessary for most of these rides. Some trails are not technically challenging and can be ridden with either a full-fledged mountain bike or an all-terrain bicycle; this is noted in the individual ride descriptions.

Cyclocomputer

A cyclocomputer will make the directions in this book easier to follow, as turns and special features are noted to the tenth of a mile. Where possible, special features or landmarks at trail turnoffs have been noted for the benefit of cyclists without computers. You can complete these rides without a computer, but the chances of getting lost or missing a side trail to a waterfall or other highlight will be increased. Variations in tire pressure, in tire size, in cyclists' weight, and in individual cyclocomputers can produce different mileage readings over identical paths. Your readings may not always agree with those provided in this book, but they should be close.

Tool Kit

Many of these trails and roads wind through remote areas of forest, so a tool kit is highly recommended. The most common mechanical problem on the trail is a flat tire. Be certain you have a bicycle pump, tire irons, and a patch kit or a spare tube with you. If you have never changed a flat tire, learn how and practice at home before your ride. And if you are mechanically inept (like me), bring along a friend who knows what a chain rivet tool and an Allen wrench are and, better yet, knows how to use them. I have seen some impressive repairs out on the trail that have kept riders riding. Even a broken derailleur doesn't necessarily mean hoofing it back to the car; the right tool and a little ingenuity can have you up and spinning again, even though you will be limited to a single gear.

First-aid Kit

Again, many of these trails and roads are in remote sections of forest where the rescue index is poor. Bring a small, well-appointed first-aid kit with you. It is also a good idea to include a stubby candle and matches in the kit. In winter, you would not want to leave an injured rider without a warming fire while you sought medical assistance.

Water

When it comes to water, I have two pieces of advice: Bring your own, and bring enough. The creeks and rivers may look pristine, but gone are the days when cyclists could dip their water bottles into a cold mountain stream for an easy refill. There are some bad bugs around, the most notable being giardia. This single-cell organism can wreak havoc in your intestines if allowed to set up residence. So how much should you bring? You know your needs better than anyone else, but take a minimum of two water bottles. For long, strenuous rides or hot-weather rides, you'll need more. Sure, extra water adds weight, but staying well hydrated is of critical importance.

Safety

The United States Forest Service makes the following recommendations for safety in the back country:

1. Always let someone know where you are going, what route you are taking, when you expect to return, and what to do if you don't.
2. Check the weather forecast; be prepared with proper clothing and equipment for all potential weather conditions.
3. Don't push yourself beyond your limits.
4. Keep an eye on each other.
5. Plot your progress on a map as you travel; know where you are at all times.

Etiquette

Mountain bikers are the new kids on the block, or rather the new kids in the woods. We must be cognizant of the rights of others in the forest and treat others with courtesy. It takes only a few discourteous, irresponsible acts of destructive riding to close a trail to mountain bikes permanently. Ride responsibly. The National Off Road Bicycle Association (NORBA) promotes the following guidelines:

1. Yield the right of way to other nonmotorized recreationists; realize that people judge all cyclists by your actions.
2. Slow down and use caution when approaching or over taking others, and make your presence known well in advance.

3. Maintain control of your speed at all times, and approach turns in anticipation of someone around the bend.
4. Stay on designated trails to avoid trampling native vegetation, and minimize potential erosion by not using muddy trails or short-cutting switchbacks.
5. Do not disturb wildlife or livestock.
6. Do not litter; pack out what you pack in, and pack out more than your share whenever possible.
7. Respect public and private property, including trail-use signs and No Trespassing signs; leave gates as you found them.
8. Be self-sufficient, and let your destination and speed be determined by your ability, your equipment, the terrain, and present and potential weather conditions.
9. Do not travel solo when "bikepacking" in remote areas; leave word of your destination and when you plan to return.
10. Observe the practice of minimum-impact bicycling by "taking only pictures and memories and leaving only waffle prints."
11. Always wear a helmet whenever you ride.

Many of the trails covered in this guide are also used by equestrians, so exercise courtesy when you encounter horses. Always dismount and give the horse the right of way. If you approach the horse from the front, dismount and stand on the side of the trail. Stay in the horse's line of vision; wait to remount until it has moved well away. If you approach a horse from the rear, dismount and walk slowly until the rider notices you. The rider should move off the trail to allow you to walk your bike past. Remount when you are well away from the horse. If the rider doesn't move off the trail, ask him how he would like you to pass so that you won't spook his horse.

Campgrounds and Accommodations

Northwest North Carolina

The following campgrounds are managed by the Grandfather District of Pisgah National Forest:

1. Boone Fork Campground (no showers)
2. Curtis Creek Campground (no showers)
3. Mortimer Campground (no showers)

For campground information, maps, and current trail information, contact:

United States Forest Service
Grandfather District, Pisgah National Forest
P.O. Box 519
Marion, N.C. 28752
(704) 652-2144

A complete listing of campgrounds, accommodations, and bike shops for the northwest North Carolina area is available through the following offices:

Boone Chamber of Commerce
208 Howard Street
Boone, N.C. 28607
(704) 264-2225

Blowing Rock Chamber of Commerce
P.O. Box 406
Blowing Rock, N.C. 28605
(704) 295-7851

Banner Elk/Linville Chamber of Commerce
P.O. Box 335
Banner Elk, N.C. 28604
(704) 898-5605

For guided tours of the northwest North Carolina area, contact:

Jo Jo Keen
Back Country Bike Tours
Route 1, Box 639
Blowing Rock, N.C. 28605
(704) 295-9815

Southwest Virginia

The following campgrounds are managed by Mount Rogers National Recreation Area:

1. Beartree Campground (hot showers)
2. Grindstone Campground (hot showers)
3. Hurricane Campground (hot showers)
4. Raccoon Branch Campground (no showers)
5. Raven Cliff Campground (no showers)

For campground information, maps, and current trail information, contact:

Mount Rogers National Recreation Area
Route 1, Box 303
Marion, Va. 24354
(703) 783-5196

A complete listing of campgrounds, accommodations, and bike shops for the southwest Virginia area is available through the following offices:

New River Trail State Park
Route 1, Box 81X
Austinville, Va. 24312
(703) 699-6778

Virginia Department of Conservation and Recreation
203 Governor Street, Suite 302
Richmond, Va. 23219
(804) 786-1712

Pulaski Chamber of Commerce
P.O. Box 169
Pulaski, Va. 24301
(703) 980-1991

Galax Chamber of Commerce
405 North Main Street
Galax, Va. 24333
(703) 236-2184

Abingdon Chamber of Commerce
179 East Main Street
Abingdon, Va. 24210
(703) 628-8141

There is an element of risk associated with the sport of mountain biking. This book is intended to serve as a guide to rides, not as a guarantee against injuries and getting lost. The author and publisher assume no liability for damages sustained by readers using this guidebook.

Life is either a daring adventure or nothing.

Helen Keller

Northwest North Carolina

<u>Boone / Blowing Rock Area</u>

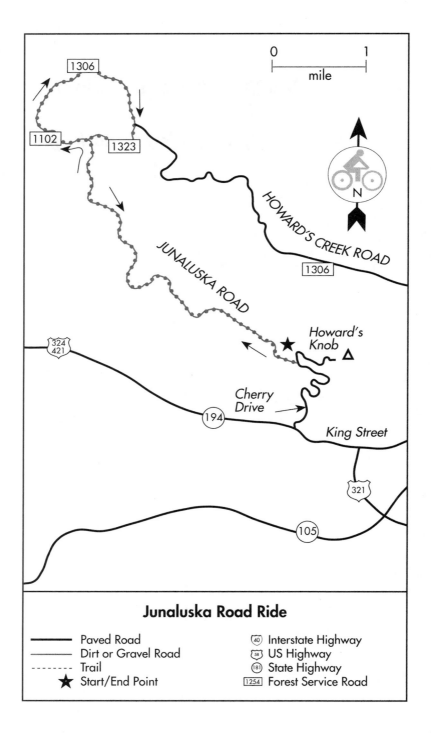

1306

1102   1323

HOWARD'S CREEK ROAD

1306

JUNALUSKA ROAD

0   1
mile

N

324
421

Howard's
Knob

Cherry
Drive

194

King Street

321

105

Junaluska Road Ride

— Paved Road
— Dirt or Gravel Road
---- Trail
★ Start/End Point

(40) Interstate Highway
(58) US Highway
(18) State Highway
1254 Forest Service Road

Junaluska Road Ride

Distance: 14 miles

Difficulty: Moderate

Riding surface: Dirt road

Maps: 1. Boone/Watauga County Map
2. USGS 7.5 minute quadrangle, Zionville. N.C.
3. USGS 7.5 minute quadrangle, Boone, N.C.

Access: From the intersection of U.S. 321 and U.S. 421 in Boone (at the historic Dan'l Boone Inn), proceed north on the combined U.S. 321/421 for about 0.1 mile. Turn right onto Cherry Drive. Follow the signs for Howard's Knob Park. At 0.2 mile, you will come to a fork in the road; bear right onto Eastbrook Drive. Almost immediately, you will have to bear left to continue. At 0.4 mile, you will come to a yield sign and a wide Y-intersection; turn right onto Hunting Road. At 0.5 mile, turn left onto Eastview Drive. At 1 mile, Old Junaluska Road is on the left; continue straight. At 1.4 miles, park at the pull-off near the turnoff for Junaluska Road (S.R. 1102), now a dirt road.

Elevation change: The ride begins at an elevation of 4,000 feet at the Junaluska Road turnoff. The elevation gain is steady but moderate, with the ride reaching a maximum of 4,300 feet at Trivett Gap. It drops to 3,800 feet, then quickly gains 400 feet on Curly Maple Road (S.R. 1323). On the return trip, there is a climb to 4,300 feet and then a gradual descent back to the 4,000-foot elevation at the end of the ride. The total elevation gain is 1,200 feet.

Configuration: Out-and-back

Sticking to hard-packed dirt roads for its entire 14-mile distance, this ride doesn't challenge cyclists with gnarly, technical single-track sections. However, it will give your heart and lungs a run for their money. And if your quad muscles aren't screaming at you at the top of the climbs, then you must have cheated and gotten a sag ride to the top.

Boone-area mountain bikers frequently train on Junaluska Road for two reasons: its physical challenge and its proximity to town. There are steady, long climbs followed by swift descents that barely give you enough time to catch your breath. There are also moderate stretches that offer you the chance for some gentle pedaling at relaxing touring speeds. Add idyllic scenery and the end result is an exceptional mountain-bike ride. And all of this within a water-bottle's throw from downtown Boone. Who could ask for anything more?

The ride begins on a wide dirt road that is in good condition. There are a few potholes and rocky hills to negotiate, but for the most part, the ride poses little technical challenge. In the first mile or so, bikers can enjoy picturesque views of nearby mountains and cattle grazing the sloping green hills and valleys. Some sections of the road are crowded with dense hardwood forests, while others are flanked by open, grassy fields. Split-rail fences, cornfields, and modest farmhouses nudge cyclists with gentle reminders of rustic civilization.

0.0 The ride begins with a left turn on Junaluska Road, now a dirt road.

2.2 You will reach an intersection of roads at Trivett Gap. On the right is the turnoff for Howard's Knob Loop. A field is on the right and a private home on the left. Continue straight.

2.7 You will come to a Y-intersection; bear right to continue.

5.3 You will come to the intersection of Junaluska Road and Curly Maple Road; bear left on Junaluska Road to continue.

Grinding up the hills of Junaluska Road

6.2 An unmarked dirt road is on the left; continue straight.

7.1 Bear right on Howard's Creek Road (S.R. 1306). (Sugarloaf Road bears left.)

7.5 Turn right onto Curly Maple Road.

8.7 Turn left onto Junaluska Road. Begin retracing your path to the starting point.

11.8 On the left is the turnoff for Howard's Knob Loop; continue straight.

14.0 At the stop sign, you will reach the starting point and the end of the ride.

Note: To increase the length of this ride to 17 miles, and to increase its difficulty rating to strenuous, you can begin cycling from the intersection of U.S. 321 and U.S. 421 in Boone. Follow the Access directions and you will grind up a hill that gains 750 feet in 1.4 exhausting miles. But there is a prize for all the blood, sweat, and tears shed on the climb: the descent waiting for you at the end of the ride.

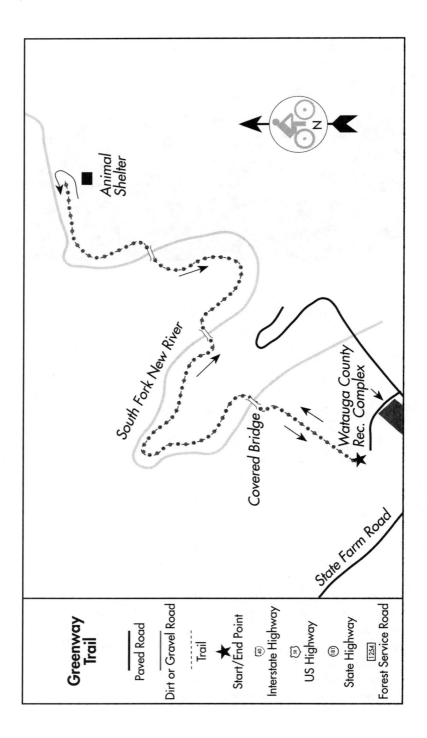

Greenway Trail

Paved Road

Dirt or Gravel Road

Trail

★ Start/End Point

🛣️ Interstate Highway

🛣️ US Highway

🛣️ State Highway

1254 Forest Service Road

N

South Fork New River

Animal Shelter

Covered Bridge

Watauga County Rec. Complex

State Farm Road

Greenway Trail

Distance: 6 miles

Difficulty: Easy

Riding surface: Gravel trail, dirt trail, dirt road

Map: Greenway Trail Map and Guide, available from Watauga County Parks and Recreation Department, 704 Complex Drive, Boone, N.C. 28607 (704-264-9511)

Access: From the intersection of U.S. 321 and U.S. 221 in Boone, drive south on U.S. 221 for 0.5 mile. Turn left onto State Farm Road. After about 1 mile, turn left into the Watauga County Recreation Complex. A large, paved parking area is located between the swimming pools and tennis courts.

Elevation change: There is no appreciable change in elevation.

Configuration: Out-and-back

This easy mountain-bike ride offers an ideal afternoon of two-wheeled recreation for families and beginners. The trail's surface consists of packed gravel and hard-packed dirt for its entire length. It is gently graded, with essentially no climbs. Though this trail seems custom-made for beginners and occasional cyclists, experienced cyclists enjoy it as well, due to its in-town location and natural beauty.

One section of the trail is especially scenic as it winds through an area dense with mature rhododendron and majestic oak trees.

For much of its length, the trail parallels the dark waters of the South Fork of the New River, which flow like molasses down the mountain. This river is considered the oldest in America, though its name would lead you to believe otherwise. It also holds the distinction of being one of the few rivers east of the Mississippi to flow northward.

With its slowly flowing waters and occasional riffles, the New River is ideal for canoe camping. Its popularity with paddlers was boosted in the mid-1970s, when a 26-mile section was designated a National Wild and Scenic River. In 1976, President Gerald Ford found a few minutes—when he wasn't busy tripping over golf balls or falling down steps—to sign the bill. And to his credit, the National Wild and Scenic River designation forever saved the New River from being dammed.

The trail crosses the river several times on wooden bridges, the first of which is a newly constructed covered bridge. Though quaint by design, this covered bridge has not yet attained the weathered finish sported by bridges in romantic locales, such as Robert James Waller's Madison County.

Wide paths offer a nice alternative to narrow single track.

When you reach the end of the trail near the animal shelter, a left turn will lead you across the river and onto Charlie Holler Road (S.R. 1515). An old cemetery located on this road may be of special interest to riders with a historical bent. Old, weather-beaten tombstones lean tiredly on a sloping, grass-covered hill. Most of the inscriptions on the stone grave markers have been muted by the forces of nature over the last 200 years, though a few are still legible. One tombstone marks the burial site of a Revolutionary War soldier.

Near the edge of the road is a rock marker informing visitors that this is also the site of the original Three Forks Baptist Church, which stood on this land in the late 1700s.

0.0 Begin cycling at the far end of the parking lot. The trail skirts the edge of the tennis courts before leaving the complex.

0.4 You will cross the South Fork of the New River on a wooden covered bridge.

1.3 You will reach the New River dam site; continue cycling the trail.

1.9 A cable strung across the trail marks the end of Greenway Trail. The animal shelter is across the road on the right; if you need to refill your water bottles, you can do so at the water fountain at the animal shelter. Turn left onto the gravel road. You will immediately cross the New River over a low-water bridge and then cycle up a short hill.

2.0 At the stop sign, turn right onto Charlie Holler Road and cycle toward the cemetery, which will be on your left.

3.0 Charlie Holler Road ends at U.S. 421. Turn around and retrace your path.

6.0 You will arrive back at the starting point.

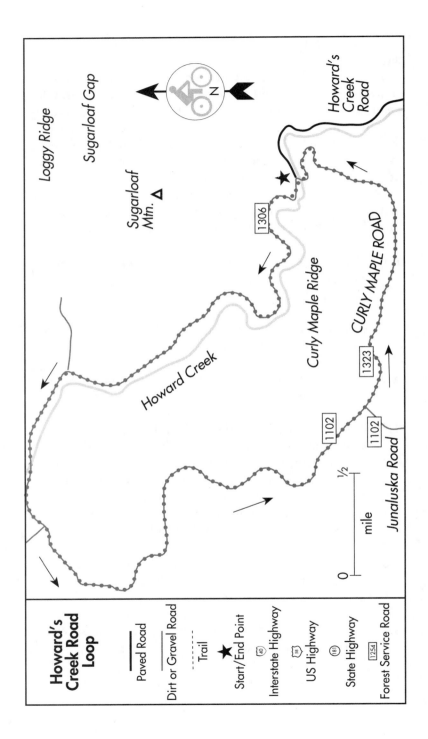

Howard's Creek Road Loop

Paved Road

Dirt or Gravel Road

Trail

★ **Start/End Point**

40 **Interstate Highway**

58 **US Highway**

18 **State Highway**

1254 **Forest Service Road**

Loggy Ridge

Sugarloaf Gap

Sugarloaf Mtn. △

Howard's Creek Road

1306

Curly Maple Ridge

CURLY MAPLE ROAD

Howard Creek

1323

1102

1102

Junaluska Road

0   ½   mile

N

Howard's Creek Road Loop

Distance: 3.3 miles

Difficulty: Easy

Riding surface: Dirt road

Maps: 1. Boone/Watauga County Map
2. USGS 7.5 minute quadrangle, Zionville, N.C.

Access: From the intersection of N.C. 194 and U.S. 221/
421 in Boone, drive north on N.C. 194. After 1.5 miles,
turn left onto Howard's Creek Road (S.R. 1306); watch
carefully for this turn. Drive 5.1 miles on this paved road
until the surface changes to dirt. Curly Maple Road (S.R.
1323) is on the left. Park on the side of the road.

Elevation change: The ride begins at an elevation of 3,800
feet and eases up to 4,000 feet in the first mile. It drops
back to 3,800 feet, only to creep up to 4,000 feet again.
You will reach the maximum elevation of 4,200 feet by
the time you turn onto Curly Maple Road. It is then a
gentle downhill roll back to the starting point on Howard's
Creek Road. The total elevation gain is 600 feet.

Configuration: Loop

Idyllic scenery on Howard's Creek Road

This loop of dirt roads offers an excellent introductory ride for beginners and once-in-a-blue-moon cyclists. Its short length, easy riding surface, and gentle grade give newcomers a chance to try out their bicycle legs without unduly challenging them. Occasional cyclists will enjoy the idyllic setting and the time spent outdoors getting a little fresh air and exercise. Experienced cyclists looking for a relaxing tour and a day off from hammering the hills will also enjoy this loop.

Though close to the town of Boone, this ride quickly transports you from the cacophony of traffic and the hordes of noisy tourists to a placid, pastoral setting. You will pedal along ribbons of hard-packed dirt past rolling countryside, farmhouses, haystacks, and occasional pumpkin patches, all of which highlight the beauty of this ride. A variety of mature hardwood trees makes this ride especially pretty in autumn.

0.0 You will begin by cycling Howard's Creek Road. This is the same road you drove in on, though its surface has changed from pavement to dirt.

0.4 Sugarloaf Road, a gravel road, is on your right. Continue straight.

1.2 You will arrive at the intersection of Howard's Creek Road and Junaluska Road (S.R. 1102). Bear left on Junaluska Road to continue.

2.2 You will arrive at the intersection of Junaluska Road and Curly Maple Road; bear left on Curly Maple Road to continue.

3.3 The dirt road ends at the intersection with Howard's Creek Road. You will arrive back at the starting point.

It's a long walk back if you don't know how to perform basic repairs on the trail.

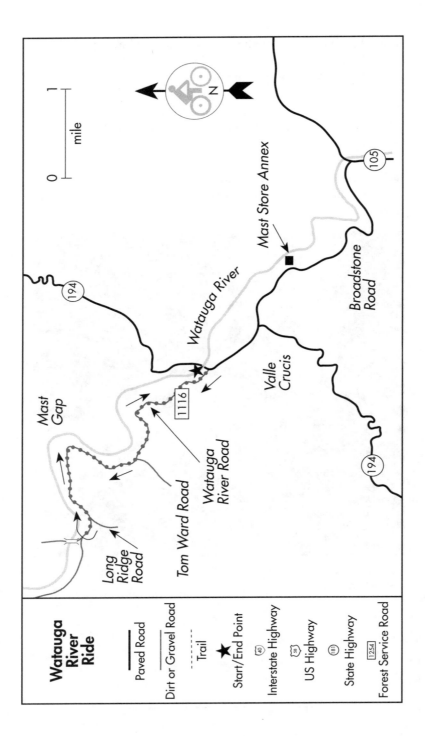

Watauga River Ride

Paved Road

Dirt or Gravel Road

Trail

★ Start/End Point

[40] Interstate Highway

[58] US Highway

[181] State Highway

[1254] Forest Service Road

Mast Gap

Long Ridge Road

Tom Ward Road

Watauga River Road

1116

Valle Crucis

Watauga River

Mast Store Annex

Broadstone Road

[194]

[194]

[105]

N

0 — 1 mile

Watauga River Road Ride

Distance: 8 miles

Difficulty: Easy

Riding surface: Dirt road

Maps: 1. Boone/Watauga County Map
2. USGS 7.5 minute quadrangle, Valle Crucis, N.C.

Access: From U.S. 321 in downtown Boone, turn onto N.C. 105 South, heading toward Linville and Banner Elk. After 4.7 miles, turn right onto Broadstone Road at the blinking lights and the sign for Valle Crucis. Drive 2.7 miles to the intersection with N.C. 194; Valle Crucis Elementary School will be on your right. Continue straight past this intersection. You will drive past the original Mast General Store, on the right. The turnoff to Watauga River Road is about a quarter-mile past the Mast General Store. If you cross the Watauga River, you have gone too far. Park at the pull-off on the right at the beginning of this dirt road.

Elevation change: The ride begins at an elevation of 2,600 feet. It reaches a maximum of 2,750 feet near the turnaround point. The total elevation gain is 150 feet, just perfect for a leisurely Sunday-afternoon bicycle tour.

Configuration: Out-and-back

Tobacco curing in a Valle Crucis barn

Easy mountain-bike rides are rather scarce in the mountain country of western North Carolina, but a gem of a ride runs along the bank of the Watauga River near the town of Valle Crucis. This nontechnical ride offers cyclists just a bit of climbing on a hard-packed dirt road that is in good condition. This ride is appealing to all cyclists, but it is especially good for beginning and occasional cyclists.

Not only does it offer a pleasant hour or two of pedaling, but it also winds through scenic pastureland. Early in the ride, slender hardwood trunks rise from either side of the road and create a natural tent over the road. Farther along, massive shoals of dark rock line the river; the rough texture of this rock abutting the smooth, indigo surface of the river creates a spectacular backdrop to the ride. Though the road tends to hug the bank of the Watauga River, there are several sections that curve away to thread through open fields. Attractive homes and cabins, some adorned with split-rail fences and landscaped rhododendron hedges, punctuate the natural beauty of the ride with a dose of upscale Valle Crucis civilization.

Two creeks flowing from opposite directions into Dutch Creek Valley form the shape of a cross and give the town its name, which means "Valley of the Cross." The valley, nestled in the lap of the mountains near Boone and Banner Elk, is quiet and remarkably beautiful. One late afternoon when my daughter and I were cycling, the serene air was especially captivating. The last light of day dimly illuminated grazing cows, creating vivid silhouettes against the black river. Regardless of whether you time your ride for sunset or earlier in the day, you are sure to find this gently rolling route quite picturesque.

The beauty of the ride is certainly enhanced by the pastoral countryside, but the Watauga River is the star of the show. The Watauga is well known by paddlers for its challenging whitewater rapids, though this placid stretch is no indication of the white-knuckle thrills boaters seek. This peaceful portion of the Watauga is known as Section II and is considered the calm before the storm. When the river squeezes through the rugged Watauga Gorge on its stunningly beautiful course to Tennessee's Watauga Lake, the excitement begins. There are several waterfalls and huge, house-sized boulders that separate the experts from the rookies and the lucky from the unlucky.

This appetizer of a mountain-bike ride will whet your appetite for the highlights found in the Valle Crucis area. While here, you might want to take in some of the many historical sights. For starters, the original Mast General Store, built in the late 1800s, is located within a stone's throw of the starting point of the ride. This old mercantile store, still very much in operation, stands in Valle Crucis as a prime example of turn-of-the-century Americana. Not surprisingly, there are quite a few historic bed-and-breakfast inns in the area, including the nationally renowned Mast Farm Inn. For more information on the history, lore, and highlights of the Valle Crucis area, you might want to pick up a copy of *Touring the Western North Carolina Backroads*, by Carolyn Sakowski.

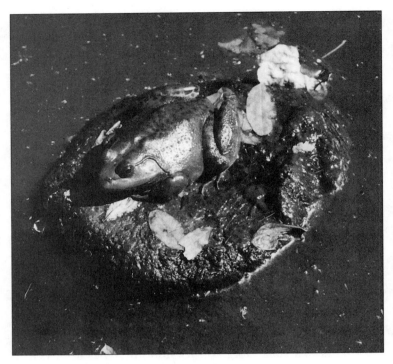

Slimy fauna found on the Watauga River

There is one special consideration to take into account before embarking on this ride. You will notice that some parts of the road are not much higher than the river at normal water levels. With any appreciable rainfall, the swollen river quickly floods the road. If you insist on cycling this dirt road during or after inclement weather, be prepared with a PFD to don over your Lycra biking attire, and perhaps outriggers to keep your mountain bike from capsizing.

0.0   Begin the ride by turning left onto Watauga River Road, a dirt road.

0.5   Dramatic rock outcroppings are to the left. Continue straight on the dirt road.

1.8 Tom Ward Road is on the left; continue straight.

3.8 Long Ridge Road is on the left; continue straight.

4.0 On the right is a bridge across the Watauga River. Turn around at this point and begin retracing your path.

8.0 You will return to the stop sign at Broadstone Road, which marks the end of the ride.

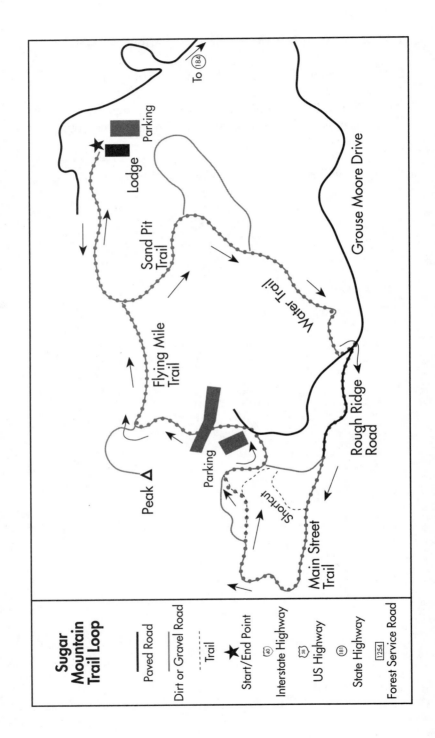

Sugar Mountain Trail Loop

Paved Road

Dirt or Gravel Road

Trail

★ Start/End Point

🛣40 Interstate Highway

🛣58 US Highway

🛣68 State Highway

1254 Forest Service Road

To 184

Parking

Lodge

Sand Pit Trail

Water Trail

Flying Mile Trail

Peak ▲

Parking

Shortcut

Grouse Moore Drive

Rough Ridge Road

Main Street Trail

Sugar Mountain Trail Loop

Distance: 5.9 miles

Difficulty: Moderate to strenuous

Riding surface: Double-track trails, single-track trails, brief sections of paved roads

Map: Mountain Bike Trail Map, available from Sugar Mountain Resort, Inc., P.O. Box 369, Banner Elk, N.C. 28604 (704-898-4521)

Access: From Linville, drive north on N.C. 105 for 3.9 miles to the intersection with N.C. 184. Turn left onto N.C. 184, heading toward Banner Elk, and drive 1.5 miles to the Sugar Mountain Resort turnoff. Turn left and drive through the main entrance. Follow the signs to the ski lodge. Park in the large parking area near the lodge.

Elevation change: The ride begins at an elevation of 4,100 feet and climbs quickly, reaching a maximum of about 5,200 feet near the 4-mile mark. From that point, there is a gradual loss of elevation until you reach the ski slopes. There, the elevation quickly drops to 4,100 feet. The total elevation gain is about 1,100 feet.

Configuration: Loop

Season: This loop is open to mountain bikers only when the ski slopes are closed. Some trails not located on the ski slopes can be ridden year-round; check with the resort for current information.

*We lost count of the number of overlooks
and great views we found on this mountain biking loop.*

Gone are the ice and snow. What's left are grassy, green slopes dotted with pale gray rocks and summer's dandelions. The ski lifts are quiet, almost ghostlike, dangling forlornly in the stillness of shimmering heat. A lonely, weather-beaten ski glove rests against a clump of grass on the slope. A buckle and a dark blue, torn piece of a bib overall strap lie across the trail. A broken ski pole sticks out of a bush, calling up an image of a frustrated, angry skier who probably was forced to descend the icy slopes with the help of only balance and luck.

This is an off-season look at Sugar Mountain Ski Resort. Though it may paint a bleak picture for skiers, it sparks the antennae of mountain bikers, who know how good riding can be on off-season ski slopes. And Sugar Mountain hasn't let cyclists down; the resort is now promoting its recently developed network of mountain-bike trails. "Sugar Is Sweet for Mountain Bikers" reads the headline of a recent article in the High Country Mountain Bike Association's newsletter. You're bound to agree.

Though it stops just short of bumping your bike computer up to a reading of 6 miles, this short ride is tough. Sugar

Mountain's special-events coordinator, Kim Schmidinger, guided me on this loop. She warned me before we shoved off that "this ride is really pretty strenuous." Hearing this from a young, athletic woman who is a retired member of the United States Women's Ski Team made me realize that I was in real trouble. I could picture myself being laid on one of those ski gurneys and hauled down the mountain by converted Ski Patrol personnel, forced to click out of their ski bindings and into mountain-bike pedals.

While the ride is certainly challenging, it wasn't quite as torturous as I'd expected. Beginning on a rocky double-track trail, it wastes no time in making you drop into your small chain ring. You may find your typical early-ride whatcha-been-up-to-lately conversations coming to a quick halt. The climbing ends at the top of the ski slope, as does the open scenery. The next leg of the loop is a narrow, rolling single-track trail tucked into a dense forest. You won't see the ski slopes again until the end of the ride.

Well marked and easy to follow, this loop offers a combination of climbs and fun, moderately technical descents. Occasional overlooks near the trails give mountain bikers panoramic vistas of nearby mountains, including those of neighboring ski resorts. Much of the ride is shady and cool, while other portions will pop you into open areas where the sun will glaze your shoulders.

Near the end of the ride, you'll have a chance to blast through a beautiful green glade shaded by occasional tall hardwood trees. Thrilling to pedal, this narrow, single-track section of trail weaves around tree trunks and visits pockets of dense foliage hiding rocks and tricky trail obstructions. In the spring, a luxuriant carpet of feathery ground cover will tickle your ankles if you drift from the center of the trail. Popping up through all this greenness are purple trillium, violets, and little daisies. Huge yellow buckeye trees tower overhead and help block out the heat. This sweet stretch of trail doesn't last long, unfortunately. You will soon be spinning along the grassy double track again.

Finally, the trail descends until it deposits you at the top of the ski slope you rode up earlier. Now it's time to go back down. No snowplowing this time of year—this is the season for fat tires. If a straight shot down the slope is a little too vertical for your taste, then do as the skiers do and traverse the slope from side to side. You can control your speed better, and the downhill grade won't be nearly so formidable.

0.0   Begin riding at the base of Sugar Mountain Resort, at the bottom of Easy Street Slope (the brown lift). Locate the green trail markers and begin following them up the edge of the slope on a rocky double-track trail. You will begin climbing immediately.

0.5   You will pass under the ski lift and come to the top of a hill; there is a nice view to the left. Turn right here. A green trail marker with an arrow shows the direction of the loop. Pedal a short distance, then turn left at the next green trail marker. You will cycle up a bank, go through an opening in the wooden fence, and then turn left at the fence. You will pedal around the red "bull wheel"—or turnaround station—of the ski lift and then begin another climb.

0.7   At the green ski lift, there is a view of Hawksnest Ski Resort to the left. You will continue straight and start descending a wide, tree-lined trail.

0.8   The Sky Leaf condominiums are on the right. The trail you are pedaling is actually an easement that allows skiers direct access to the slopes during winter.

0.9   You will pedal into a sandy clearing. Continue following the green trail markers, heading straight on a level-to-descending single track. This is called Sand Pit Trail.

1.3   You will come to an intersection with a trail with yellow markers. Turn right and begin following the yellow trail makers. (If you go straight, you will come to a pump house.) You can hear a stream trickling

Some parts of Sugar Mountain Trail Loop pass right under the ski lift.

through the woods. After this turn, you will begin climbing on a double-track trail with a moderately technical surface of gravel and dirt. This is called Water Trail. You will pass several pump houses along the way.

1.8   The trail ends at Grouse Moore Drive, a paved road. On the left are the Misty Woods condominiums. Continue following the yellow trail markers by turning left onto Grouse Moore Road, then immediately right onto Rough Ridge Road. You will descend on this rough-textured paved road.

2.3   The pavement ends. Continue straight on a double-track trail with a gravel and dirt surface. This is Main Street Trail. Continue following the yellow trail markers. At this point, you can see Linville Ridge on the left. Horse stables are located on fenced private property on the left. On the right is a trail with orange markers, a difficult technical climb.

2.6   You will intersect a shortcut for the trail with orange markers. Continue straight, following the yellow trail markers.

3.3   You will reach a narrow single-track trail on the left that leads to a beautiful overlook. You may want to walk this short distance for a view of Beech Mountain and other surrounding mountains and valleys.

3.4   Turn right onto a narrow single-track trail not yet marked with colored trail signs. You will immediately come to a fork; turn left.

3.9   You will return to the grassy road. Turn right and descend, following the yellow markers. (To the left, the grassy road dead-ends at the peak of Sugar Mountain; you may want to visit this overlook if you can spare the energy.)

4.3   You will intersect the trail with orange markers; continue straight.

4.4   The trail ends at Grouse Moore Drive, a paved road; turn left.

4.5   Turn left at the Sugar Ski and Country Club sign. The Sugar Top condominiums loom off to the right.

4.6   Turn left at the stop sign and follow the yellow trail markers through the parking lot of the condominium complex. At the bottom of the parking lot, turn left and begin pedaling across the ski slopes again. There is a cable strung across the beginning of this double-track trail; this is Cat Trace Trail. On the right is a good view of Hanging Rock and the surrounding mountains.

4.8   You will come to an intersection of trails; turn right. (If you continue straight, the trail will lead you to a great view at the top of Sugar Mountain.)

Purple trillium thrives along some of the single-track sections, making a late spring ride especially enjoyable.

4.9 At the yellow ski lift, turn left and follow the wide, grassy path on the right side of the slope. This stretch of the loop is steep, technical, and full of potholes that will send you over your handlebars if you're not careful. When Kim Schmidinger guided me on this trail, we traversed the grassy ski slopes on the way down the mountain, rather than plunging down the grass road. This made the descent easier and was a lot of fun.

5.9 You will return to the starting point at the main lodge building.

Note: Sugar Mountain Resort is the first ski resort in the Boone/Banner Elk area to develop mountain-biking trails as part of its efforts to attract vacationers year-round. The resort doesn't charge a fee to ride the trails, but it does require that cyclists wear helmets. So if you want to be an organ donor, you'll have to ride without a helmet elsewhere.

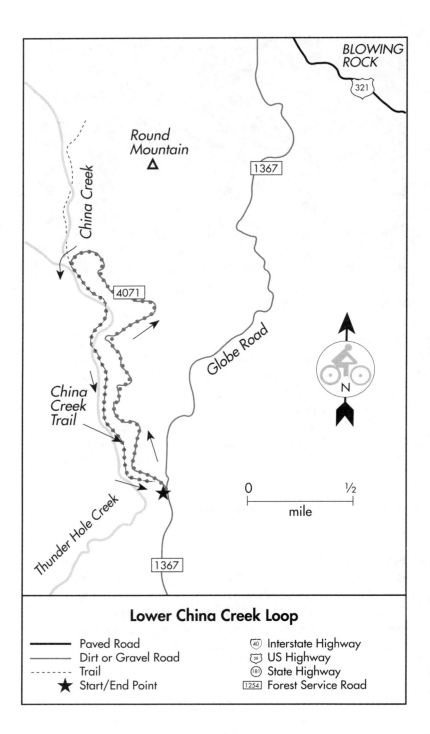

Lower China Creek Loop

▬▬▬ Paved Road	⓪ Interstate Highway
─── Dirt or Gravel Road	Ⓢ US Highway
------- Trail	⑱ State Highway
★ Start/End Point	1254 Forest Service Road

BLOWING ROCK

321

Round Mountain
▲

1367

China Creek

4071

Globe Road

China Creek Trail

Thunder Hole Creek

0   ½
mile

N

1367

Lower China Creek Loop

Distance: 3.9 miles

Difficulty: Easy

Riding surface: Dirt road, single-track trail

Maps: 1. Pisgah National Forest: Grandfather District
2.USGS 7.5 minute quadrangle, Globe, N.C.

Access: From the junction of U.S. 321 and U.S. 221 in Blowing Rock, drive south on U.S. 321 Business for 0.4 mile. Turn right onto Globe Road (S.R. 1367) and drive approximately 3.2 miles to a pull-off on the right next to F.R. 4071. Park here.

If you like, you can start this ride in Blowing Rock and increase the total distance by about 7 miles. Globe Road is hot and dusty in the summertime, however.

Elevation change: The ride begins at an elevation of about 1,750 feet and climbs steadily along the dirt road to a maximum of about 2,000 feet at the intersection with China Creek Trail. It drops back to 1,750 feet on its return to the starting point. The total elevation gain is 250 feet. However, if you pedal from Blowing Rock, you will gain about 1,750 feet on the way back into town. That's quite a hump in just 3.5 miles!

Configuration: Loop

Try doing this with a skinny-tired racing bike!

Short and sweet, this mountain-bike loop offers an ideal ride for beginners and cyclists just looking for an hour's spin in the woods. It is so close to Blowing Rock that you can almost see the trailhead from Main Street. The ride can be lengthened and the difficulty increased by pedaling straight from town and humming down Globe Road to the turnoff. You will have a grind of a climb back into town, though, gaining 1,750 feet of elevation in only 3.5 miles.

Half the loop is on a forest-service road that curls up toward the junction of China Creek and Thunderhole Creek. The other half is on a beautiful stretch of descending single track that flirts with the banks of Thunderhole Creek. There are several frigid creek crossings that will take your breath away if you fail to negotiate them successfully. Mountain bikers have given the creek's name new meaning, their cries thundering through the forest after an icy spill.

Creatures on two wheels aren't the only varmints you're likely to run into on this trail. You might see a cobalt blue salamander sunning itself on a smooth, gray river rock, or a friendly garter snake working on its tan. Cock an ear to the forest and you might hear a squirrel foraging for nuts or birds at play. My friend Owen Riley and I came upon two shrews noisily darting about in the dry leaves. When they glanced up and saw us peering down at them, they hastily abandoned their game and bolted for cover. And though we never saw any, these dense woods are filled with white-tailed deer, wild turkey, and grouse.

0.0 You will begin pedaling a dirt road that starts with a gradual climb.

1.5 You will cross New Year's Creek.

2.1 China Creek Trail crosses the road. Turn left and pedal down China Creek Trail.

2.4 You will cross Thunderhole Creek.

2.5 You will cross Thunderhole Creek again.

Don't scream—it's just a friendly little garter snake catching some rays.

3.7 The trail ends at the dirt road; turn right to return to Globe Road.

3.9 You will arrive back at the starting point.

Zipping down the single track

Pisgah National Forest

Wilson Creek Area

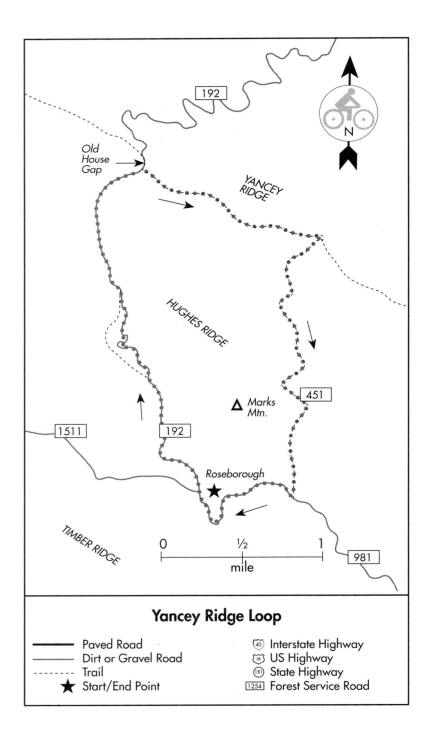

192

Old
House
Gap

YANCEY
RIDGE

N

HUGHES RIDGE

△ Marks
Mtn.

451

1511

192

Roseborough

★

TIMBER RIDGE

981

0   ½   1
              mile

Yancey Ridge Loop

▬▬▬ Paved Road	ⓐ Interstate Highway
──── Dirt or Gravel Road	ⓢ US Highway
----- Trail	⑱ State Highway
★ Start/End Point	1254 Forest Service Road

Yancey Ridge Loop

Distance: 8.2 miles

Difficulty: Moderate to strenuous

Riding surface: Dirt road, four-wheel-drive road

Maps: 1. Wilson Creek Area Trail Map
2. USGS 7.5 minute quadrangle, Grandfather Mountain, N.C.

Access: From the intersection of U.S. 221 and N.C. 105 in Linville, drive south on U.S. 221. After approximately 0.2 mile, turn left onto Roseborough Road (S.R. 1511); this is the second left after the intersection of U.S. 221 and N.C. 105. Roseborough Road is paved until it reaches the Blue Ridge Parkway after 1.6 miles, where the surface changes to dirt. As you continue on Roseborough Road, you will be descending through scenic surroundings. Rattlesnake Cliffs loom over the road at the 3-mile mark. Some 6.7 miles from the traffic light in Linville, you will arrive at a dirt parking area which marks the beginning of the ride.

Elevation change: This loop begins at an elevation of 2,000 feet. It steadily climbs to 3,000 feet by the turnoff at Old House Gap, then reaches a maximum of 3,100 feet before it levels off and begins descending. By the turnoff to Marks Mountain, the elevation drops to 2,600 feet. The road continues on a gently descending grade, reaching 2,400 feet at F.R. 981. This dirt road will return you to the starting point and an elevation of 2,000 feet. The total elevation gain is 1,100 feet.

Configuration: Loop

The Wilson Creek area has long been regarded by local mountain bikers as a haven for off-road cycling. Its popularity is just beginning to extend beyond the local cycling community. In response to the area's growing reputation as a premier destination for mountain biking, the rangers of the Grandfather District of Pisgah National Forest are currently working to designate more single-track trails for mountain-bike use. To help in this endeavor, a Boone-area biking club, the High Country Mountain Bike Association, has worked diligently with the forest service by clearing and maintaining trails.

Though only two single-track trails are currently designated for mountain-bike use, there are myriad other ride possibilities in the Wilson Creek area. Miles and miles of gated forest-service roads wind through these beautiful, green mountains. Fortunately, mountain bikers are welcome to pedal all of these dirt roads. Though many such narrow dirt tracks are classified as roads, most cyclists would be hard-pressed to describe them as anything other than *trails*.

Yancey Ridge Loop, probably the most popular of all Wilson Creek's mountain-bike rides, is a perfect example. This moderately strenuous loop consists of old logging roads and four-wheel-drive roads, though you would swear that you're on single-track trails for much of the ride.

The ride begins on F.R. 192, a gently climbing dirt road flanked by towering hardwood trees. The woods are punctuated by stately hemlock trees rising from an understory of dark green rhododendron. After a mile or so of steady climbing, the grade steepens to a strenuous grind up the west side of Hughes Ridge. If you have not worked up a sweat by the time you reach the turnoff at Old House Gap, then you must be dead.

The climb continues for a short distance on the four-wheel-drive road on top of Yancey Ridge, but it soon subsides. This old logging road has suffered from erosion; the ditches left behind will thrill hammerhead cyclists. When I rode this trail, the hard-core mountain bikers in my group loved this technically challenging section. They dropped into the furrows in the road, pulled their knees and elbows close to their bodies, and pedaled away. The rest of us dismounted and pushed our bikes, offering all kinds of pitiful excuses—down to a sore throat—for not riding this extremely technical section.

If you manage to lift your eyes from the rocky, technical trail unrolling before your wheels, there are occasional spots along the ridge top that offer glimpses of the nearby mountains. These beautiful views all but disappear during summer, when the hardwoods are at their verdant, leafy finest.

The ride continues with a right turn onto F.R. 451, which drops down the east side of Marks Mountain. This is a fast, fun leg offering some logs to jump or bunny-hop and some technical sections to negotiate. A final right turn onto F.R. 981 brings the loop to a close.

0.0 From the parking area at the end of the road, turn right and pedal across a low-water concrete bridge. Take the first left onto a wide dirt road.

3.0 At Old House Gap, turn right and pedal uphill; at this turn, you will see an old, dilapidated wooden gate on the right that is partially buried in the ground.

4.5 Turn right onto F.R. 451, a four-wheel-drive road.

7.1 Turn right onto F.R. 981, a wide, well-groomed dirt road.

8.2 You will arrive back at the starting point.

Don't tell me that we are lost again!
Photo by Owen Riley, Jr.

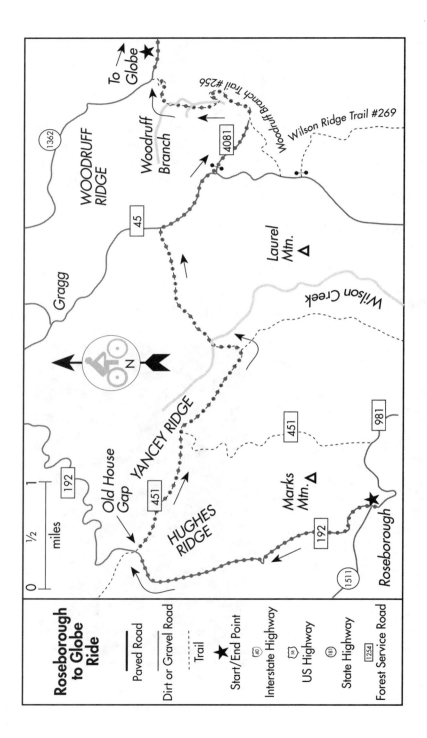

Roseborough to Globe Ride

Paved Road
Dirt or Gravel Road
Trail
★ Start/End Point
⑩ Interstate Highway
⑱ US Highway
⑱ State Highway
1254 Forest Service Road

To Globe ★

Woodruff Branch Trail #256

Wilson Ridge Trail #269

WOODRUFF RIDGE

Woodruff Branch

1362

4081

45

Gragg

Laurel Mtn. △

Wilson Creek

N

192

Old House Gap

YANCEY RIDGE

451

HUGHES RIDGE

451

981

Marks Mtn. △

192

1511

Roseborough ★

miles
0   ½   1

Roseborough to Globe Ride

Distance: 14.1 miles

Difficulty: Moderate to strenuous

Riding surface: Dirt road, single-track trail, paved road

Maps: 1. Wilson Creek Area Trail Map
       2. Pisgah National Forest: Grandfather District
       3. USGS 7.5 minute quadrangle, Grandfather
          Mountain, N.C.
       4. USGS 7.5 minute quadrangle, Globe, N.C.

Access: To reach the Roseborough access, drive south for approximately 0.2 mile on U.S. 221 from the intersection of U.S. 221 and N.C. 105 in Linville. Turn left onto Roseborough Road (S.R. 1511), the second left after the intersection of U.S. 221 and N.C. 105. Roseborough Road is paved until it reaches the Blue Ridge Parkway at 1.6 miles, where the surface changes to dirt. As you continue on Roseborough Road, you will be descending on a very scenic dirt road; Rattlesnake Cliffs loom over the road at the 3-mile mark. At 6.7 miles from the traffic light in Linville, you will arrive at a dirt parking area, which marks the beginning of the ride.

To reach the Globe access, drive south on U.S. 321 Business for 0.4 mile from the junction of U.S. 321 and U.S. 221 in Blowing Rock. Turn right onto Globe Road (S.R. 1367) and drive approximately 8 miles to the end of the road. Globe Baptist Church is straight ahead. Turn right and park at the pull-off on the right next to the creek.

Elevation change: This ride begins at an elevation of

2,000 feet in Roseborough. It steadily climbs, reaching 3,000 feet at the turnoff at Old House Gap. The ride then levels off and begins descending, though there are still a few hills thrown in to keep you honest. The elevation drops to 2,000 feet at Wilson Creek. A climb follows as the trail heads toward F.R. 45 and an elevation of 2,500 feet. At the gated turnoff to Woodruff Branch Trail, the elevation is 2,600 feet and the climbing is over. You will drop to 1,350 feet by the time you reach your shuttle vehicle in Globe. The total elevation gain is about 1,600 feet.

Configuration: One-way

This level, hard-packed trail will put a smile on any mountain biker's face.

This is one of the classic mountain-bike rides in the high country of western North Carolina. Though "classic mountain-bike ride" tends to conjure up images of places like Moab and Tsali, where there are hordes of cyclists and wall-to-wall Lycra and titanium, this ride doesn't fall into that category. Though local cyclists often pedal this route, I have yet to see another group of riders out spinning along when I have been on these trails. Solitude seekers, you had better enjoy it while you can. There's no way a gem of a ride like this will remain in the shadows.

You will start pedaling on F.R. 192 right in the teeth of a pretty tough climb. You will gain 1,000 feet of elevation by the time you pedal into Old House Gap, only 3 miles from the starting point in Roseborough. Make friends with your small chain ring, because you will be intimate with it for several long stretches on this ride.

You will then turn onto F.R. 451, a moderately technical four-wheel-drive track. You will do some climbing, but it is the descents you will remember later. You can plunge straight down the great downhills on this stretch for a thrilling ride. Or you can weave from side to side as David Dauphiné of Blowing Rock does, carving brisk turns on the basin-shaped banks of the road. I can't remember the last time I saw a grown man have such a good time with his clothes still on. I believe that David squeezed every last drop of fun out of that descent.

As good as this four-wheel-drive path is for mountain biking, just wait until you zip down the technical single track that spills into Wilson Creek. The trail might not be the only thing spilling into the creek, because the rocks are slippery. In all, members of my group made about a dozen attempts to pedal through the water, but the slick rocks got us every time. The opposite side of the creek is a jumble of large boulders, perfect for propping up your soggy feet to dry them out. What follows is a tough, technical climb that seems to last forever. A stretch of exquisite single track waits, so hunker down, pedal on, and get this climb over with.

Woodruff Branch Trail is a single-track treasure. Fallen pine needles blanket the trail and muffle the sound of spinning tires. The smell of flowering trees such as Fraser magnolias occasionally wafts over you as you pedal. White pines crowd the trail and reach out to tickle and prick your bare arms as you blast through the woods.

If you think it just can't get any better than this, think again. You are about to pedal down to a rushing waterfall tucked away in a pocket of pristine wilderness. A tranquil pool shimmers at the base of the fall and might just lure you in for a dip on a hot summer day.

The final leg of this exceptional ride is along Anthony Creek Road, a dirt road that changes to pavement. Rolling countryside fans out on either side of the road, and azalea farms, tree farms, and nurseries dot the landscape. Nearby Avery County is renowned as a shrubbery capital, and these small farms seem to have spread from that major hub. There are no climbs and no descents on this road. It is just a peaceful stretch of pavement that offers a perfect ending to one of the best mountain-bike rides in northwest North Carolina.

Mountain biker and best friend just before falling into Wilson Creek

0.0 After leaving a shuttle vehicle in Globe, begin this ride in Roseborough. From the parking area at the end of the road, turn right and pedal across a low-water concrete bridge. Almost immediately, take the first left onto F.R. 192, a wide dirt road.

3.0 At Old House Gap, turn right and pedal uphill. This wide jeep track is F.R. 451.

4.7 Another jeep road is to the right; continue straight.

5.1 There is a logging road on the left marked with a yellow-painted gatepost. Bear right at this fork to continue.

5.6 There is a clearing on the left. A spring is located here. If you need to refill water bottles, look for the pipe in the ground.

6.0 A four-wheel-drive road is on the right; continue straight.

7.0 You will make a hard left at the bottom of the hill onto a descending single-track trail.

7.3 The trail turns right and sends you down a steep, technical track. It then turns right again.

7.5 You will cross Wilson Creek. This creek crossing is a walker. After crossing, turn left and push your bike through some boulders to continue.

7.6 After pushing up a rocky slope, you will come out onto a grassy trail; a little cabin is straight ahead. Turn right to continue.

7.8 There is a chimney on the left, followed by a creek crossing.

7.9 You will pedal across another stream. There are a few cabins and shacks along the way.

8.0 You will cross a creek.

8.2 You will cross another creek.

8.8 You will come to a gate across the trail. Pedal around it and continue straight.

8.9 Turn right onto F.R. 45, a gravel road. Some small houses and shacks are in this area.

9.7 There is a single-track trail on the right that climbs a hill. On the left is a gravel logging road that is gated. Turn left onto this gravel road.

10.5 The gravel road swings left, and Woodruff Branch Trail (#256) crosses the road. Turn left onto this narrow single-track trail marked with a red, round blaze.

10.8 The trail crosses a gravel road; continue straight across the road. Continue following the red, round blazes.

11.0 The trail ends on a technical, steep stretch spiced with water bars. Turn right onto the gravel road, pedal about 50 feet, and then turn left to return to Woodruff Branch Trail.

11.3 The trail makes a sharp right turn. On the left is a delicate, cascading waterfall.

11.6 You will pedal across a creek. The remnants of a stone chimney are on the right.

11.8 You will pedal across a creek.

11.9 The trail surface changes to rock. On the left are the headwaters of a waterfall.

12.0 You can hike a short distance down to a beautiful 25-foot waterfall. At the base of the fall is an inviting pool you might want to cool off in during summer.

12.2 You will reach the end of Woodruff Branch Trail. Turn right onto Anthony Creek Road (S.R. 1362), a gravel road.

12.7 The gravel road changes to pavement. On the left is Rackett Creek Place (S.R. 1361); continue straight on Anthony Creek Road.

14.1 You will arrive in Globe, which marks the end of the ride.

Woodruff Branch Waterfall—a pleasant highlight toward the end of the ride

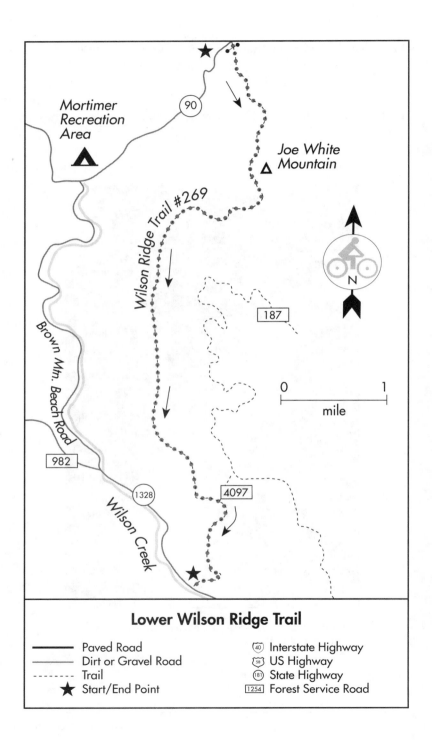

Mortimer
Recreation
Area

⛺

90

Joe White
Mountain
△

Wilson Ridge Trail #269

Brown Mtn. Beach Road

187

982

1328

4097

Wilson Creek

N

0   1
mile

Lower Wilson Ridge Trail

——— Paved Road
——— Dirt or Gravel Road
------- Trail
★ Start/End Point

㊵ Interstate Highway
㊿ US Highway
⑱ State Highway
1254 Forest Service Road

Lower Wilson Ridge Trail

Distance: 8.6 miles

Difficulty: Moderate to strenuous

Riding surface: Single-track trail, old logging road, dirt road

Maps: 1. Wilson Creek Area Trail Map
2. Pisgah National Forest: Grandfather District
3. USGS 7.5 minute quadrangle, Collettsville, N.C.

Access: To reach the S.R. 90 access, drive south approximately 0.2 mile on U.S. 221 from the intersection of U.S. 221 and N.C. 105 in Linville. Turn left onto Roseborough Road (S.R. 1511), the second left after the intersection of U.S. 221 and N.C. 105. Roseborough Road is paved until it reaches the Blue Ridge Parkway at 1.6 miles, where the surface changes to dirt. Drive 8.8 miles until you reach the T-intersection with S.R. 90. Turn right and drive 2 miles to Mortimer Recreation Area. Continue on S.R. 90 another 2.5 miles; the gated, old logging road which is the Lower Wilson Ridge trailhead is on the right. Though there is no trail signpost, a blue triangle is nailed to a tree on the right.

To reach the Brown Mountain Beach access, follow the above directions to Mortimer Recreation Area. Turn onto Brown Mountain Beach Road (S.R. 1328) and drive 4 miles to the bridge across Wilson Creek. Continue straight for another 1.9 miles to the end of Wilson Ridge Trail, which is on the left. There are some large rocks at the end of the trail and a blue triangle on a tree. Leave your vehicle at any of the many pull-offs near the trail.

Elevation change: The trail begins at an elevation of 2,200 feet and climbs quickly to 2,600 feet. After a few dips, it climbs Joe White Mountain to an elevation of a little more than 2,800 feet. A descent to 2,400 feet follows before the climbing resumes. The trail reaches nearly 2,600 feet again, then makes a final drop to a minimum of 1,300 feet. The total elevation gain is 800 feet.

Configuration: One-way

Pedaling past early blooming mountain laurel is a real treat.

Feel robust? Feel like a little two-wheeled exploration? Feel like pulling out the ol' compass and map and trying to figure out just where the heck you are? Well, maybe you won't have to do all that, but I know someone who greeted nightfall while still out on Wilson Ridge Trail. Fortunately, the moon was full, so he was able to negotiate his way along the trail with some degree of certainty. And since it was a clear night, he was able to guide himself by the stars to where he thought he needed to go. By the time he popped out onto paved road after 11:00—he was supposed to be at the end of the trail by

6:00, tops—he had clocked 26 miles on his cyclometer, rather than the estimated 8 or 9 miles. And this was an experienced outdoorsman.

If you have a tendency to get lost, better try another ride in this guidebook. Though the High Country Mountain Bike Association has worked hard to mark and clear this trail, there are still some sections that are pretty darn tricky. Rather than the trees being blazed with colored paint, blue triangles have been nailed to them to mark the route. These triangles don't exactly jump out when you are pedaling along at breakneck speed. There are also some significant turns that might be hard to notice even if they were marked with blinking neon signs.

Your first time on this trail, you might consider checking with some of the Boone bike shops or the High Country Mountain Bike Association to see if you can join a planned ride. Or find someone who knows the trail well, and go with that person. Or try dropping breadcrumbs to find your way out, but we all know where that landed Gretel. At the very least, make sure that you or someone in your group has the topographical maps for this ride, as well as a compass. A bike computer will also greatly help in following the directions in this chapter. Getting lost in these hills is a real possibility. Just ask my husband.

For those of you who haven't been scared away, let me say that despite the nebulous nature of this route, this is really a great mountain-bike ride. Even though it is less than 9 miles long, this trail is a true challenge. In a nutshell, this is a ride of extremes: extreme climbs, extreme downhills, and extreme beauty.

Some of the climbs are straight-up grinds, while others are stairstep ascents. Some of the downhills are simple plunges, while others are downright wild. Whipping through the forest around bends on technical, deeply rutted, nearly vertical surfaces is like paddling a kayak into the Chattooga River's infamous Bull Sluice rapid. Well, not quite. But it is thrilling, just the same. If you're looking for gentle climbs and easy downhills, then you'd better look elsewhere, for the mountains of Wilson Ridge are going to sock it to you.

On a tamer note, Wilson Ridge Trail is as aesthetically

pleasing as it is heart-pounding. The trail weaves through dense forests of oak, hickory, and maple, dotted with a variety of wildflowers during the warm months. Columbine, wild iris, and fire pinks—to name just a few—are prolific along the trail. The blossoms of mountain silverbell trees and the fuzzy yellow flowers of sweetleaf trees will bathe your nose with their sweet fragrances as you pedal past.

Leaving the woods, the trail occasionally shoots into open clearings that offer expansive views of nearby mountains and valleys. At the upper end of the trail, you will see a mountain off to the right that looks like the dorsal fin of a shark. This is Table Rock Mountain, the giant stone chameleon of Pisgah National Forest. You can view this mountain from north, south, east, and west, and its appearance will be different from each vantage.

0.0   After leaving a shuttle vehicle at the end of the trail on Brown Mountain Beach Road, begin the ride on S.R. 90. Cycle around the gate and up the grassy, old logging road.

0.2   You will come to a clear-cut section. Bear right and pedal across this open area and then up a raw dirt slope.

0.3   You will enter the woods on a climbing single-track trail.

1.1   On a descent, the road swings to the right. You will continue descending.

1.5   There are posted signs on either side of the trail. Stay on the trail and off this private property.

2.1   A white cabin is on the right; continue straight.

2.4   A single-track trail is on the left. There is a cable strung across an old logging road on the right. Continue straight through a mature stand of poplar trees.

2.7 There is a private drive on the left marked with a red gate. Just past this drive, you will pedal around a huge mud puddle in the trail. Cables are strung between trees on either side of the trail. Just past these cables are double blue triangles nailed into a tree on the right; these indicate a change of direction. Turn left onto a narrow, rutted, climbing single-track trail. If you miss this turn, you will come to a closed red gate just around the bend.

2.9 There is a beautiful view on the left.

4.2 A very large tree lies across the trail. There is a path on the left that horses have made when going around this obstruction.

Taking a break after a tough climb

Picking a line on a technical stretch of single track

5.4 You will come to a clear-cut area on the left which offers pretty views. A huge hemlock tree is on the left. Turn left here onto a steeply descending single-track trail. You will see a blue triangle on a tree as soon as you turn. This is a tricky, hidden turnoff; be watching for it or you will miss it.

5.8 You will come to a gravel clearing. A descending gravel road is on the right. Continue straight on the trail.

6.1 You will negotiate a steep descent. Turn left onto the gravel road at the bottom of the hill.

6.3 The trail departs the gravel road to the right to climb a ridge. Continue straight and stay on the road.

6.7 There is a single-track trail on the right that climbs a steep bank. A nice overlook is on the right. Continue straight on the road.

7.1 You will arrive at a T-intersection. Turn right onto the gravel road.

7.4 You will reach a gravel turnaround. A climbing gravel road bears right; it dead-ends. You will need to bear left onto a narrow single-track trail and descend.

8.1 You will come to a T-intersection; turn right to continue.

8.6 The trail ends at Brown Mountain Beach Road.

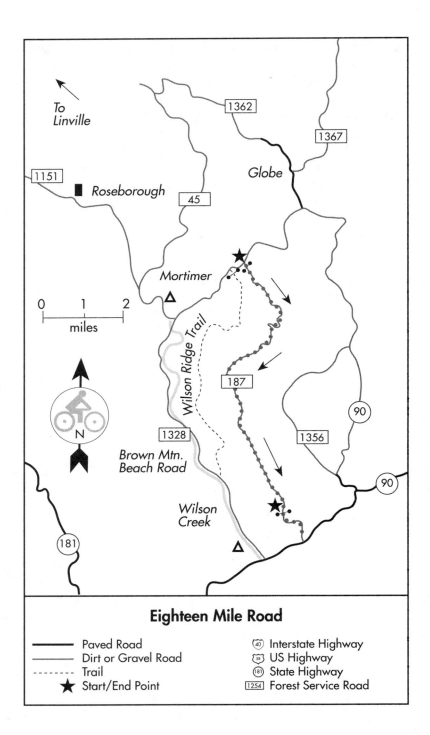

To
Linville

1362

1367

1151

Roseborough

Globe

45

Mortimer

△

Wilson Ridge Trail

0   1   2
miles

N

187

90

1328

1356

Brown Mtn.
Beach Road

Wilson
Creek

90

△

181

Eighteen Mile Road

— Paved Road
— Dirt or Gravel Road
---- Trail
★ Start/End Point

40 Interstate Highway
38 US Highway
181 State Highway
1254 Forest Service Road

Eighteen Mile Road Ride

Distance: 16.9 miles

Difficulty: Moderate

Riding surface: Dirt road

Maps: 1. Pisgah National Forest: Grandfather District
2. Wilson Creek Area Trail Map
3. USGS 7.5 minute quadrangle, Collettsville, N.C.

Access: To reach the upper access, drive south on U.S. 221 for approximately 0.2 mile from the intersection of U.S. 221 and N.C. 105 in Linville. Turn left onto Roseborough Road (S.R. 1511), the second left after the intersection of U.S. 221 and N.C. 105. Roseborough Road remains paved until it reaches the Blue Ridge Parkway after 1.6 miles, where the surface changes to dirt. Drive 8.8 miles until you reach the T-intersection with S.R. 90. Turn right and drive 2 miles to Mortimer Recreation Area. Continue on S.R. 90 for about 3.5 miles to the intersection with F.R. 187; Maple Grove Baptist Church is located at this intersection. Park at any pull-off.

To reach the lower access, follow the above directions to Mortimer Recreation Area. Turn onto Brown Mountain Beach Road (S.R. 1328) and drive about 8.5 miles to the end of the road. Turn left onto Adako Road (S.R. 1337), a paved road. After about 1.3 miles, turn left onto Murphy Place Road (S.R. 1407). Drive 1 mile to F.R. 187. Leave your vehicle at any pull-off near this intersection.

Elevation change: The elevation at the beginning of the ride is 2,200 feet. It drops for the majority of the ride, though there are some hills thrown in for flavor along the way. The total elevation gain is 600 feet.

Configuration: One-way

Thrill seekers may scoff at a day spent mountain biking a forest-service road, but this gated dirt road offers a thrill that no single track can match. And that is speed. There are no tight, off-camber, hairpin turns to slow you down, no logs to jump, no sections so steep and technical that you have to stop and pray before plunging headfirst into a green abyss. And with the aid of a mountain biker's best friend—the closed gate—there is also no traffic forcing you to slow down. Without question, single-track trails are great. What mountain biker doesn't love them? But there is no way that you can clock the same speed on a trail that you can on a wildly descending, gated dirt road.

This particular forest-service road also offers exceptional scenery. It snakes through dense deciduous forests highlighted by

The views are great from F. R. 187.

The combination of beautiful scenery and winding dirt roads makes this an outstanding mountain-bike ride.

occasional patches of evergreens. Flowering trees—Carolina silverbells, dogwoods, and Fraser magnolias—embellish the highland woods during late spring. Mountain creeks sing off in the distance, and a range of wildflowers colorfully dots the hills.

A variety of animals also live in these woods. Grouse, squirrels, wild turkeys, black bear, and white-tailed deer are some of the critters you might see slipping through the forest. At some point, you will probably see a tree blazed with three orange marks. These are black-bear sanctuary markers. Thankfully, I have yet to see Smokey or any of his brethren.

However, I did have a close encounter with a small doe one Sunday afternoon while pedaling this road. I rounded a sunlit bend and came upon her feeding in some tall grass on the edge of the road. She immediately lifted her head to cast her

Bluets are common along moist creek banks in the spring.

big brown eyes in my direction. I stopped and she stopped. Here we were, two curious girls in an eye-to-eye standoff. Instead of crashing through the brush with her white flag waving good-bye, she stood still and stared right through me. I guess that I was too far away to be a threat, or else she was accustomed to Lycra-clad mountain bikers by now. Bored, she finally wandered off slowly and disappeared in the trees.

The road traces ridge lines for most of its distance, winding to scenic overlooks created by loggers. On clear days, you can see for miles across the valleys and gaps to distant knobs, hills, and mountains. Though I don't fashion myself a tree-hugging environmentalist, I do cringe when I see a familiar patch of lush, green forest obliterated by timber harvesters. But as Woody Keen of Blowing Rock says, "Look at the great views they give us!"

0.0 After leaving a shuttle vehicle at the lower end of F.R. 187, begin pedaling at the intersection of S.R. 90 and F.R. 187. Turn onto F.R. 187 and pedal around the gate.

0.4 There is a pull-off on the left. You can park here if the gate is open.

1.6 A gated road is on the right; continue straight.

3.2 A single-track trail is on the right; continue straight.

4.2 There is an ungated gravel road on the right; continue straight. F.R. 187 makes a screaming left turn.

5.3 A single-track trail is on the right.

10.1 An ungated, old logging road is on the right; continue straight.

10.4 You will come to a fork in the road; bear right on the high road to stay on F.R. 187.

Keep yourself and your dog well hydrated.

13.0 A gated road is on the right; continue straight.

14.6 There is a single-track trail on the left; continue straight.

15.7 A single-track trail is on the right; continue straight.

15.8 There is a single-track trail on the left; continue straight.

16.9 F.R. 187 ends at the T-intersection with Murphy Place Road. This marks the end of the ride.

Pisgah National Forest

Linville Gorge Area

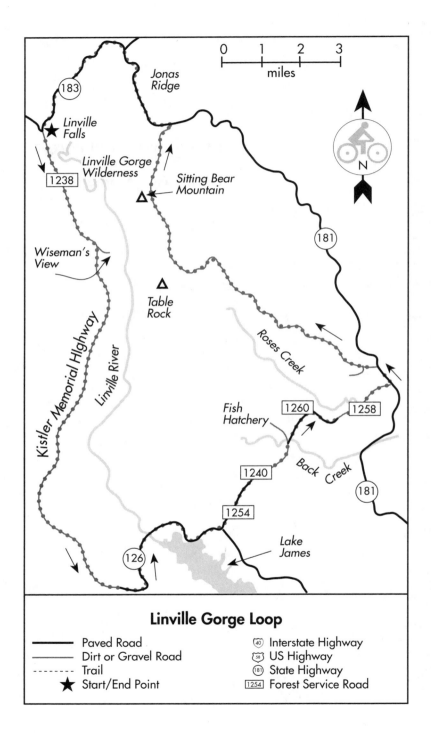

Linville Gorge Loop

—— Paved Road	⊕ Interstate Highway
—— Dirt or Gravel Road	⊕ US Highway
----- Trail	⑱ State Highway
★ Start/End Point	1254 Forest Service Road

Jonas Ridge

183

Linville Falls

Linville Gorge Wilderness

1238

Sitting Bear Mountain

181

Wiseman's View

Table Rock

Kistler Memorial Highway

Linville River

Roses Creek

1260

1258

Fish Hatchery

1240

Back Creek

181

1254

126

Lake James

0 1 2 3 miles

N

Linville Gorge Loop

Distance: 49 miles

Difficulty: Extremely strenuous

Riding surface: Dirt roads, paved roads

Maps: 1. Pisgah National Forest: Grandfather District
2. USGS 7.5 minute quadrangle,
Linville Falls, N.C.
3. USGS 7.5 minute quadrangle, Ashford, N.C.
4. USGS 7.5 minute quadrangle, Oak Hill, N.C.
5. USGS 7.5 minute quadrangle,
Chestnut Mountain, N.C.

Access: From U.S. 221 in the town of Linville Falls, turn onto N.C. 183 and drive 0.7 mile to the turnoff to the Linville Falls parking area. Park in this unpaved lot.

Elevation change: The ride begins at an elevation of about 3,300 feet at the Linville Falls parking area. It reaches a maximum of 3,950 feet on Kistler Memorial Highway (S.R. 1238) before dropping to 3,550 feet at the turnoff to Wiseman's View. The road drops to 3,000 feet and climbs to 3,400 feet before the final descent to N.C. 126 begins; by the time Kistler Memorial Highway intersects the paved road, the elevation drops to 1,400 feet. Next, the ride drops to 1,200 feet before climbing to 1,300 feet at the intersection with Fish Hatchery Road (C.R. 1254). It then drops to 1,150 feet at the N.C. 181 turnoff. From that point, the dirt road steadily climbs up to and past Table Rock Picnic Area until it reaches 3,600 feet at the Gingercake community. At N.C. 181, the elevation drops to 3,450 feet.

Another climb follows, this time to 3,800 feet. The last few miles of the ride are on a descending grade, as N.C. 183 drops back to the Linville Falls parking area. There is one final 100-foot gain between the Linville River Bridge and the Old N.C. 105 turnoff. The total elevation gain is 4,050 feet.

Configuration: Loop

N early 50 incredibly strenuous miles long, this mountain-bike ride is the longest and toughest described in this guidebook. When I was trying to rate the difficulty of various rides, this one went out of the ballpark. Without a doubt, this challenging loop is sure to peg the needle of your endurance meter.

Though the miles alone are enough to qualify this ride as strenuous, the challenge doesn't stop with distance. There are quite a few hills to tackle, to the tune of more than 4,000 feet of elevation gain. Even if you are strong, young, and a high-gear snob, you will never make it up some of these steep hills without some serious low-ring action.

And then there are the downhills. These descents are not just technical, they are scary. If you are faint of heart, weak of knee, or short on braking power, you will never make it. Sharp, screaming turns on steep grades combined with extremely technical surfaces make a recipe for a wipeout if ever there was one. Though adrenaline junkies will find it thrilling, some of you will have white-knuckle grips on your brake levers as you negotiate these drops.

There are occasional easy drifts in the ride that will give you a chance to catch your breath before the next punch. These respites may keep you from hurling your bike and yourself into the gorge, but it's the steep stuff you will remember when the ride is over.

If you can hang in there, the rewards are great, for this mountain-bike ride is as beautiful as it is difficult. The route winds around the perimeter of the Linville Gorge Wilderness, with numerous overlooks along the way affording spectacular views.

Linville Gorge is formed by Linville Mountain on the west and Jonas Ridge on the east. The ride consists of dirt roads flanking the gorge and a few brief sections of paved road connecting the eastern and western legs of the loop. Though I normally kick and scream when I have to pedal paved roads on my mountain bike, I have never been happier than when I saw blacktop on this ride. After grinding up the tough hills and negotiating the steep descents on the dirt roads, you may find yourself dropping to your knees and kissing the asphalt.

Slicing through this splendid wild country is the pristine Linville River, which thunders for 14 white, riotous miles through the gorge. It drops several thousand feet before finally calming down and draining into Lake James. The Cherokees called the river *Eeseeoh*, meaning "river of many cliffs." As you gaze at the rugged, sheer cliffs soaring 1,000 feet from the lush, green basin of the river, *Eeseeoh* will indeed seem a perfectly appropriate name.

Tucked within this canyon are pockets of virgin forest, some of the few remaining in the United States. These areas are so inaccessible that early timber speculators couldn't take trees from the backwoods coves. Axes and saws could be brought in, but the loggers had no way to haul out their woody spoils.

Views of the walls of Linville Gorge are great from Kistler Memorial Highway.

Then, in 1951, the prospect of future timber harvesting ended when the Linville Gorge was designated a Wilderness Area. Later, this area became one of the original regions covered by the National Wilderness Act. These 7,600 acres are now forever protected. As stated in the act, the Linville Gorge is among those areas "where the earth and its community of life are untrammeled by man, where man himself is a visitor who does not remain." Amen.

Mountain bikes are strictly prohibited in designated Wilderness Areas, but with the aid of the dirt roads skirting the rim of the gorge, cyclists can at least steal a peek into the basin. As you pedal, you will have views of such highlights as Table Rock Mountain, which was used by the Cherokees as a site for their sacred ceremonies. You will also enjoy a view of Hawksbill Mountain, considered by many to be more striking than Table Rock Mountain. Another highlight is Wiseman's View, named for Lafayette "Uncle Fete" Wiseman. This spot on the canyon rim was supposedly one of his favorite campsites for grazing his cattle in the mountain grasses many years ago. Another popular site is Lettered Rock Ridge, located near the turnoff to Table Rock on the eastern edge of the gorge. As the story goes, the marks on the rock are Indian letters painted by the Cherokees in the late 1700s.

Even without these highlights, the beauty of this ride would still take your breath away. Glistening green rhododendron leaves color the edges of the winding dirt roads year-round. The bushes are especially scenic in the summer, when they are heavy with pale pink blossoms.

Autumn rides in the mountains are memorable, with crisp air stirring the brightly colored leaves of the ridge-top hardwoods and finally bringing that long-awaited chill to your bare arms. And of course, there is nothing like gazing up at an autumn sky so blue that it makes you wince.

If you pedal this route on a blustery spring day, you will probably never forget it. As winds blow across the canyon walls, the resulting roar across the mountaintops is incredible.

The four-wheel-drive requirements of these dirt roads weed out Sunday drivers and dramatically reduce your chance of encountering passing vehicles. Though this is good for the sake

Kistler Memorial Highway descends to Lake James.

of solitude, you are on your own if you have a mechanical breakdown or an injury or run out of food or water. This is a long, difficult ride without any sag vehicles or stores along the way to assist you. You need to be prepared with ample water and food to last all day. Your bike needs to be in good shape, with well-adjusted, fresh brake pads. If your brakes are beginning to get a little thin, replace them before you head for this ride. You'll be glad that you did. A tool kit and a first-aid kit are also essential. This is an all-day ride, so you will need to get an early start. But most of all, don't overestimate your abilities and physical conditioning. If you are not physically up to this ride, you may find out the hard way that natural selection is still alive and well and hard at work in these hills.

0.0 Begin cycling up Kistler Memorial Highway, a dirt and gravel road.

0.4 There is an information center on the right; continue straight.

3.8 F.R. 458 is on the left. This 0.3-mile dirt road leads to Wiseman's View. (See the Wiseman's View Ride for a description of this overlook.)

5.7 There are good views of the walls of the gorge on the left.

7.3 You will hit a brief paved section of road.

12.7 There is an excellent view of Lake James on the left.

13.6 You will cycle through a community of small houses. Where there are country houses, there are also dogs, so watch out. From my experience, I have concluded that the value of country property is inversely proportional to the size and ferocity of the watchdog.

14.0 Paddy Creek Road (S.R. 1237) is to the right; continue straight.

Table Rock Mountain looms over a peaceful farm setting.

15.5 You will arrive at a stop sign at the intersection of Kistler Memorial Highway and N.C. 126, a paved road. Turn left onto N.C. 126. After the dirt-road workout, the smooth surface and downhill grade of this paved leg of the loop will look like heaven.

17.9 You will pedal across a one-lane bridge over the Linville River. Expect to see a flannel-clad trout fisherman or two planted in the cold water.

19.3 Lake James is on the right. There are some good picnic and resting spots here.

20.4 Turn left onto Fish Hatchery Road, a paved road.

21.0 You will arrive at a Y-intersection. Pea Ridge Road bears right, while Fish Hatchery Road continues straight, changing to a dirt surface and becoming C.R. 1240. To continue the loop, descend on C.R. 1240.

23.5 You will pedal across a one-lane bridge over a creek. Table Rock Mountain is visible to the left across a field.

23.7 You will arrive at a Y-intersection. Bear right on Fish Hatchery Avenue (C.R. 1260), a paved road. Do not bear left on C.R. 1240.

24.8 You will cycle past Mountain Grove United Methodist Church, established in 1860.

25.2 Turn left onto Rose Creek Road (F.R. 1258), a gravel road.

26.3 You will pedal across a one-lane bridge over Rose Creek.

Watch out for dogs!

27.3 Turn left onto N.C. 181, a paved road.

28.1 Turn left onto Simpson Creek Road (C.R. 1263), a gravel road.

28.3 Turn right at the Table Rock Picnic Area sign.

37.4 Table Rock Picnic Area is on the left at F.R. 210-B; continue straight.

41.9 You will enter the Gingercake community.

42.8 You will arrive at a yield sign; continue straight.

43.1 Turn left onto N.C. 181, a paved road.

45.1 Turn left onto Buckeye Hollow Road.

45.2 Turn left onto S.R. 1267, a dirt road.

46.9 Turn left onto N.C. 183, a paved road.

47.9 You will pass under the Blue Ridge Parkway.

48.4 You will pedal over the Linville River Bridge.

48.9 Turn left onto Old N.C. 105.

49.0 You will arrive back at the starting point at the Linville Falls parking area.

Make sure that you are in good shape or these hills will get you.

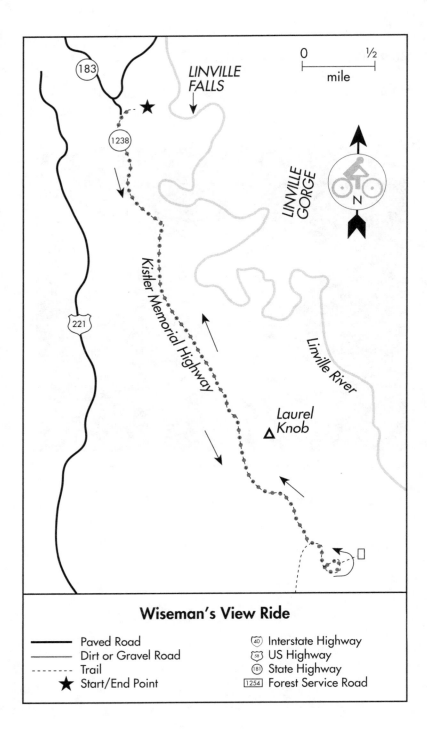

Wiseman's View Ride

―――― Paved Road	ⓐ Interstate Highway
―――― Dirt or Gravel Road	⑤ US Highway
-------- Trail	⑱ State Highway
★ Start/End Point	☐1254 Forest Service Road

183

1238

LINVILLE FALLS

LINVILLE GORGE

N

221

Kistler Memorial Highway

Linville River

Laurel Knob

0 ½
mile

Wiseman's View Ride

Distance: 8.2 miles

Difficulty: Moderate

Riding surface: Dirt road

Maps: 1. Pisgah National Forest: Grandfather District
2. USGS 7.5 minute quadrangle,
Linville Falls, N.C.

Access: From U.S. 221 in the town of Linville Falls, turn onto N.C. 183 and drive 0.7 mile to the marked turnoff to the Linville Falls parking area. Park in this unpaved parking lot to begin.

Elevation change: The ride begins at an elevation of 3,300 feet at the Linville Falls parking area. It gains elevation slowly at the beginning, then rapidly intensifies. You will reach a maximum of 3,950 feet before the turnoff to Wiseman's View. The elevation drops to 3,400 feet by the time you reach the parking loop at Wiseman's View. The return trip involves a climb back up to 3,950 feet before the ride drops to 3,300 feet at the starting point. The total elevation gain is 1,200 feet.

Configuration: Out-and-back

View of Table Rock through the trees

Folks claim that on dark nights in these mountains, they occasionally see flickering lights darting and dancing on the hills of Brown Mountain. These lights, which have aroused curiosity for hundreds of years, were written about as long ago as the late 1700s by Gerard de Brahm, the first white man to explore this region. Indian mythology also makes mention of the mysterious Brown Mountain Lights.

The most-repeated legend explaining the lights was passed on by a Civil War veteran who served under Robert E. Lee. The soldier told of a low-country planter who became lost while hunting in the mountains. A worried slave came to the hills to try to find him and was seen searching for the man for many days. He even continued his search at night by lantern light. As the legend goes, the old slave died without ever finding his master, but his ghost still searches, and the light from the lantern still glows. Who was this Civil War veteran given credit for passing down the legend through the years? It was Lafayette Wiseman, the man for whom Wiseman's View is named.

When you pedal up to the overlook and gaze across the wilderness from Wiseman's View Trail, you will see the same view that Lafayette Wiseman saw so many years ago. Brown Mountain is visible, of course, as well as the sharply contoured Hawksbill Mountain and Table Rock Mountain. And even though you can't see it, the Linville River thunders for 14 miles through the wilderness, dropping nearly 2,000 feet in a rushing torrent of white water. It slices through the wild, rugged gorge, pinched between sheer rock walls rising high above it.

If the sights from Wiseman's View don't take your breath away, it's probably because there's no breath left in your lungs after the strenuous climb to the overlook. Simply because it sticks to dirt roads for its entire length does not mean that this is a cream-puff tour. Get ready, because this is a fairly tough mountain-bike ride. The climbs are straight-up grinds, and the descents are amazingly difficult. The surface of the road is extremely technical, due to moguls, deep ruts, and holes nearly deep enough to bury bodies. The turns are tight and sharp and will have you squeezing your brakes for all they're worth. You single-track purists might change your mind about dirt-road mountain biking after pedaling this baby.

Mountain bikes are strictly prohibited in the Linville Gorge Wilderness, but this ride offers incredible bird's-eye views of the gorge from the dirt roads along the canyon's rim. As far as scenery goes, it just doesn't get much better than this. The ride weaves through a gorgeous green setting of huge rhododendron thickets, mature hardwoods, and pines. You won't know what to expect around the next bend in the road. Pedaling through these remote backwoods tends to make you feel like you are all alone. But remember, this road is open to traffic. Be alert at all times for passing vehicles, particularly on the sharp turns when descending.

Some portions of the road are adorned with oak trees whose limbs lace together. In winter, the branches look like the arthritic hands of a wispy old woman. In summer, they provide a leafy canopy of blessed shade.

Regardless of the time of year you cycle this trail, you are sure to find beautiful highlights. Spring decorates the forest with blooming dogwoods and the brilliant orange blossoms of flame azaleas. The summer forest is scrubbed in pale pink from rosebay rhododendron blossoms. Autumn is a celebration of vibrant oranges, yellows, and reds that seem to set the forest on fire. And winter soothes the eyes with the clean beauty of slender, gray, leafless hardwood trunks rising amid dark evergreens.

0.0 Begin cycling Kistler Memorial Highway (S.R. 1238), a dirt and gravel road.

0.4 An information center is on the right; continue straight.

0.8 There is a large parking area on the left at the Pine Gap trailhead; continue straight. Don't forget that Linville Gorge Wilderness is off-limits to mountain bikes. If you stray from the dirt road onto any of the single-track trails leading down into the gorge, you'll go straight to hell when you die. Don't say you weren't warned.

Pedaling a gentle section of Kistler Memorial Highway

1.5 There is a parking area on the left at a single-track trailhead; continue straight.

1.6 A pretty view of the gorge is on the left; continue straight.

1.7 A pull-off and overlook of the gorge are on the left; continue straight.

1.9 There is a parking area on the left at the Cabin trailhead; continue straight.

2.4 You will begin a very technical descent.

2.7 There is a parking area on the left at the Babel Tower trailhead; continue straight.

3.8 Turn left onto F.R. 458, a pine-bordered dirt road leading to Wiseman's View.

4.1 You will arrive at the parking loop for Wiseman's View. The 0.2-mile Wiseman's View Trail is for hikers only; mountain bikes are prohibited on it. After taking in the views, turn around and begin retracing your path.

4.4 Turn right onto Kistler Memorial Highway.

8.2 You will arrive back at the starting point at the Linville Falls parking area.

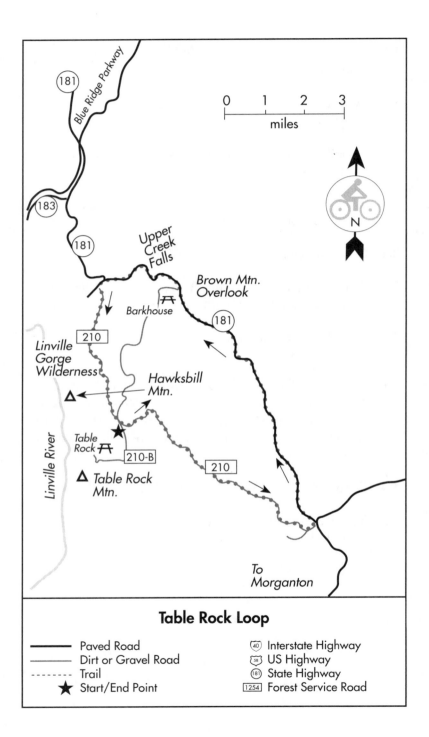

181

Blue Ridge Parkway

183

181

Upper Creek Falls

Brown Mtn. Overlook

Barkhouse

181

210

Linville Gorge Wilderness

Hawksbill Mtn.

△

Table Rock

210-B

210

△ Table Rock Mtn.

Linville River

To Morganton

Table Rock Loop

——— Paved Road
——— Dirt or Gravel Road
--------- Trail
★ Start/End Point

(40) Interstate Highway
(58) US Highway
(181) State Highway
1254 Forest Service Road

0   1   2   3
miles

N

Table Rock Loop

Distance: 26.2 miles

Difficulty: Strenuous

Riding surface: Dirt road, paved road

Maps: 1. Pisgah National Forest: Grandfather District
2. USGS 7.5 minute quadrangle,
   Linville Falls, N.C.
3. USGS 7.5 minute quadrangle,
   Chestnut Mountain, N.C.
4. USGS 7.5 minute quadrangle, Oak Hill, N.C.

Access: From the intersection of N.C. 181 and N.C. 183 south of Linville, drive south on N.C. 181 for approximately 3 miles to the turnoff for Gingercake Road (S.R. 1264); there is a sign at this turnoff showing the mileage to Table Rock Picnic Area. Turn right and drive 0.3 mile to a fork in the road. Bear left on Gingercake Acres Road, which becomes F.R. 210; the road changes from pavement to dirt. Drive 5.4 miles to the turnoff to Table Rock Picnic Area at F.R. 210-B. You can either park at a pull-off near this intersection or drive nearly 3 miles up F.R. 210-B to Table Rock Picnic Area and park there. Since there is limited parking at the picnic area, it is best to park elsewhere on pretty weekends, when the area is heavily used. Starting at the picnic area adds about 6 miles to the ride.

Elevation change: The ride begins at an elevation of 2,600 feet at the intersection of F.R. 210 and F.R. 210-B. It descends to 1,150 feet by the turnoff for N.C. 181. Then the climbing begins. You will pedal to an elevation of 3,450 feet by the turnoff for Gingercake Road and reach a maximum of 3,600 feet within the next mile. You will lose about 1,000 feet in the next 4 miles back to the starting point. The total elevation gain is 2,450 feet.

Configuration: Loop

Hills, hills, and more hills . . .

It's either up or down on this ride, with very few level spots in between. Starting off with a descent, you will bomb down a beautiful forest-service road that winds through dense forests of white pine, spruce, and oak. Occasional flashes of silver will grab your attention, as sparkling mountain streams trickle through basins filled with hemlock and rhododendron. The scenery is gorgeous and the descent is thrilling, but there is work to do. Fighting gravity is a tough job, but somebody's got to do it. And the task begins on N.C. 181.

This is a monster climb—2,300 feet of elevation gain in a measly 11 miles. But it could be worse. The paved surface makes the climbing constant, with no interruptions—like a washboard surface or potholes—to mess up your rhythm. Technical expertise is not required to crest this climb, but endurance and strength are essential. This is a great transition loop for experienced road cyclists interested in trying on a mountain bike for size. The paved portion of road is steep, but the extra gears on a mountain bike help a lot.

For some cyclists, hill climbing is a head game, a sort of Zen experience. Steady pedaling seems to free you of the petty distractions of everyday life. You forget about the proposal you have to make next Thursday; you forget about the weird pinging sound your car engine started making last week; you forget about the bills piling up on your desk. For now, you are only aware of the flickering specks of granite flowing beneath your slowly rolling front wheel and the burning of your quads. If you need a mantra for these hills, pick up Luka Bloom's *Acoustic*

Motorbike CD and cue it up to the title song. The tune and chorus are sure to surface in your mind on long hauls like these.

As the miles and hours pile up, you will need to stop and refuel. Bonking is a distinct certainty if you don't replace spent carbohydrates along the way. Be sure to pack sports bars, fig bars, or other snacks, and eat them before you start getting hungry. There are some inviting places along the way to stop if you need the rest—Brown Mountain Overlook, Barkhouse Picnic Area, and Upper Creek Falls, to name a few. If you can spare the energy, you can also take a round-trip hike of about a mile and a half to Upper Creek Falls; the trail is for foot travel only, so lock up your bike and hoof it.

The climbing ends, as all climbing does. Fueled with the knowledge that the work is over, you will make a swift descent on the winding dirt road that leads back to Table Rock. You'll be exhausted and drained, yet mildly giddy.

There is something about these strenuous rides that keeps us coming back for more. Maybe it's the sense of accomplishment that draws us back. Maybe it's the rush of endorphins we get from extended aerobic exercise. Or maybe it's just the thought of a cold beer buried in a cooler of crushed ice. Whatever the source, you know the feeling. And it's awfully good.

Heavily forested dirt roads are perfect for mountain-bike rides.

0.0 From the intersection of F.R. 210 and F.R. 210-B (which leads to Table Rock Picnic Area), begin cycling south on F.R. 210.

9.1 Turn left onto Simpson Creek Road (C.R. 1263), a gravel road.

9.3 Turn left onto N.C. 181, a paved road.

9.5 Brown Mountain Beach Road (S.R. 1328) is on the right; continue straight.

10.6 Steele Creek Park and Campground are on the left; continue straight.

11.2 Daniel Boone Campground is on the right; continue straight.

11.8 You will enter Pisgah National Forest.

18.1 There is a parking area on the right for Upper Creek and Greentown trails; continue straight.

18.6 Barkhouse Picnic Area is on the left.

19.4 Upper Creek Falls is on the right.

19.5 You will leave Pisgah National Forest.

20.5 Gingercake Road is on the left. There is a sign showing the distance to Table Rock Picnic Area (8.5 miles). Turn left here.

20.8 You will come to a fork in the road; bear left onto Gingercake Acres Road, which becomes F.R. 210.

26.2 You will arrive at the turnoff to Table Rock Picnic Area at F.R. 210-B and the starting point.

Pisgah National Forest
Boone Fork Area

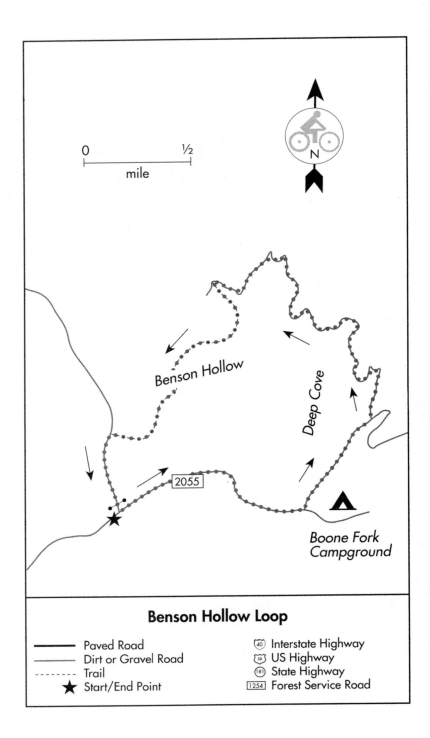

0   ½
mile

N

Benson Hollow

Deep Cove

2055

Boone Fork
Campground

Benson Hollow Loop

— Paved Road
— Dirt or Gravel Road
---- Trail
★ Start/End Point

(40) Interstate Highway
(58) US Highway
(181) State Highway
[1254] Forest Service Road

Benson Hollow Loop

Distance: 5.3 miles

Difficulty: Easy to moderate

Riding surface: Dirt road, old logging road, single-track trail

Maps: 1. Pisgah National Forest: Grandfather District
2. USGS 7.5 minute quadrangle, Globe, N.C.
3. USGS 7.5 minute quadrangle, Buffalo Cove, N.C.

Access: From Blowing Rock, drive south on U.S. 321 for 13.3 miles. Turn right onto Roby Martin Road (S.R. 1349). After 1.5 miles, the pavement ends and Roby Martin Road becomes a gravel road; continue straight. At 2.5 miles, you will come to a fork; bear right to continue. You will come to a stop sign at 4.2 miles; turn right onto S.R. 1368, a paved road. At 7.2 miles, you will see a sign for Boone Fork Recreation Area; turn right onto F.R. 2055, a dirt road leading to the campground. There is a gated road on the left at 1 mile; park at any nearby pull-off. Do not block the gate.

Elevation change: The ride begins at an elevation of about 1,250 feet and gradually climbs to 1,400 feet at Boone Fork Campground. It gains an additional 200 feet on the logging road before beginning to drop on the single-track trail. At the dirt road near the end of the loop, the elevation drops to 1,350 feet. It continues to drop, finally reaching 1,250 feet at the starting point. The total elevation gain is 350 feet.

Configuration: Loop

Streams and creeks are numerous in the Boone Fork Area.

Are you tired of old man winter's frosty fingers stroking the back of your neck? Are you sick of pulling on layer after layer of polypro and pile before hitting the trails? Are you unable to stand one more ride so cold that you have to wiggle into those bulky winter gloves that make your fingers as useless as if they were shot up with Novocaine?

As scenic as winter mountain biking is in the high mountains of North Carolina, even the most tolerant cyclist can become a little weary of the frigid temperatures. But there's a lovely area south of Boone and Blowing Rock that is substantially warmer than the high-elevation hills. Welcome to Boone Fork.

When blustery winds and subfreezing temperatures prevail in the northern reaches of Pisgah, the rides in the Boone Fork area hold great appeal for cyclists. The elevation difference of several thousand feet remarkably affects the mercury in thermometers. Also, the low-lying hollows in this area tend to hang onto the warmth, due to their natural protection from bone-chilling winds. But when summer arrives with its baggage of heat and humidity, mountain bikers take flight and migrate back to the cooler northern hills.

There are a number of ride possibilities in this area of Pisgah National Forest, including this very popular loop. If you pitch a tent in the campground, you can cycle straight from your zippered front door to begin this ride. Dirt roads, single-track trails, climbs, descents, stream crossings, pretty views, beautiful flora—this loop offers just about everything that a mountain biker could want, *and* at relatively comfortable temperatures.

Your warmup begins on a gradually climbing dirt road leading to Boone Fork Campground. You'll make a left turn onto another dirt road, this one gated and overgrown with green vegetation in the spring and summer. Fraser magnolias, holly, hemlock, and rhododendron grow in the moist soil of the thick deciduous forest flanking the road. Farther up the ridge, deciduous azaleas flourish in the drier, more acidic soil. Spring comes early on this low-elevation loop; expect to see blooms here first.

After turning off the old logging road, you will pedal along a lush, green single-track trail that leads down into Benson Hollow. Once you enter this verdant Eden, you'll feel almost like you are riding through a bowl filled with sunshine. A luxuriant ground cover of turkey feet carpets this low-lying area. Mountain streams sparkle when shafts of sunlight hit their trickling waters, creating a dazzling sight.

Then it's back out of this green glade and onto an open dirt road again. It won't be long until you catch sight of a gate across the road, which, unfortunately, marks the end of the ride.

0.0 From the parking pull-off, cycle up the dirt road leading to the campground. You will pass a popular fishing lake on the left.

1.0 You will pedal into Boone Fork Campground. Bear left onto a dirt road and cycle around the gate.

Mountain biking is great in the Boone Fork area.

1.3 You will come to a fork in the road; bear left.

2.7 Turn left onto a single-track trail which begins at a perpendicular angle to the dirt road. There are logs stacked on either side of the trail. You will know you have missed the trail turnoff if the dirt road enters a clear-cut area; the road then swings to the right and its surface changes to grass.

2.9 Continue following the trail as it bends to the right and then makes a hard right turn. There is a large stump at the turnoff.

3.0 You will cross a stream on a small log bridge.

3.1 The trail looks like it ends at the creek, but it continues on the other side. A short distance past the creek, the trail makes a hard right turn. There is a stream paralleling the trail after the turn. You will cross another stream.

3.2   You will pedal across a creek and into a deep thicket of rhododendron.

3.3   You will pedal across another stream. The trail continues on the other side, downstream a bit.

3.4   You will come to another creek crossing.

4.7   You will pedal across an old cattle guard.

4.9   You will see a National Forest Property Boundary sign.

5.0   The trail intersects a dirt road; turn left.

5.3   Pedal around the gate and return to the starting point.

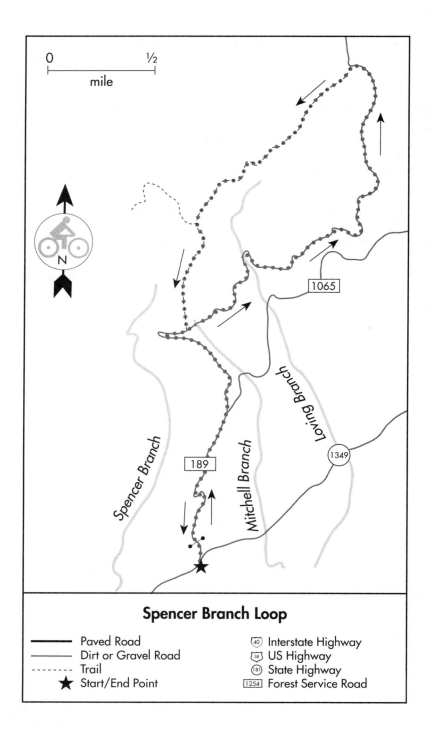

0   ½
mile

N

1065

Loving Branch

Spencer Branch

Mitchell Branch

189

1349

Spencer Branch Loop

——— Paved Road
——— Dirt or Gravel Road
- - - - - Trail
★ Start/End Point

⑩ Interstate Highway
🛡 US Highway
⑱ State Highway
☐1254 Forest Service Road

Spencer Branch Loop

Distance: 8.2 miles

Difficulty: Moderate

Riding surface: Dirt road, single-track trail

Maps: 1. Pisgah National Forest: Grandfather District
2. USGS 7.5 minute quadrangle,
Buffalo Cove, N.C.
3. USGS 7.5 minute quadrangle, Lenoir, N.C.

Access: From Blowing Rock, drive south on U.S. 321 for 13.3 miles. Turn right onto Roby Martin Road (S.R. 1349). At 1.5 miles, the pavement ends and Roby Martin Road becomes a gravel road; continue straight. At 2.5 miles, you will come to a fork; bear right to continue. Spencer Branch Road (F.R. 189) is on the right at 2.8 miles. Park at any pull-off near the beginning of this dirt road. Do not block the gate.

Elevation change: The ride begins at an elevation of 1,300 feet and steadily climbs to 2,300 feet by the turnoff at the meadow. There are a few more brief climbs, but the ride is mostly descending at this point. Toward the end of the ride, the elevation drops to 1,600 feet at the intersection of the trail and the road. A final drop on the forest-service road returns you to an elevation of 1,300 feet. The total elevation gain is 1,000 feet.

Configuration: Loop

Winding up and around the steep-sided ridge lines, this forest-service road will lead you into a remote backwoods setting that is perfect for a mountain bike. The climbing is relentless for about 4 miles, but the natural scenery helps divert your attention. Purple flowering locust bushes creep up from the banks to peer out at the road. The springtime blossoms of Fraser magnolias, Carolina silverbells, and other flowering trees send fragrant vapors drifting through the forest. The quiet reverie may be pierced by the staccato, hollow hammering of a woodpecker in the distance.

This dry, sun-parched road cuts through a grid of single-track trails and overgrown, abandoned logging roads that will leave you anxious to investigate more of the Boone Fork area. According to Jo Jo Keen of Blowing Rock, the Boone Fork area is an especially good mountain-biking destination in the winter, due to its relatively warm temperatures. This loop is located at an elevation several thousand feet lower than Wilson Creek and other northern areas of Pisgah, which tends to nudge temperatures up quite a bit. In fact, this ride's maximum elevation is less than the elevations at the starting points of some rides.

Some of these single-track trails are quite technical.

The climbing ends and the fun begins when you pedal into a meadow half-enclosed by a wall of pines. Turning left onto an abandoned jeep track, you will pedal up to a grassy knoll and then down a stretch of single-track trail. Your descent begins on a narrow path that can barely be seen as it trickles through a riotous tangle of pale green brush. The trail then slips into a forest, where it is protected from being overtaken by undergrowth; the canopy of mature, tall trees filters the sunlight and discourages the growth of understory.

The trail will disappear again, though this time not into briers and brush. The late-autumn leaf drop creates a deep sea of dry, sepia-tinted leaves that obscures the trail. As my friends and I tried to pedal through, we were quickly hub-deep in the crackling, deep piles and were abruptly halted. Attempting to ride was so difficult and so deafening that we finally just broke down in exasperated laughter. Of course, I couldn't *hear* any laughter over the din of crunching leaves, but judging from the other bicyclists' facial expressions, they appeared to be laughing.

Remember the sound effects you produced as a kid by sticking playing cards on your bicycle spokes with clothespins? Well, imagine attaching playing cards to every spoke, rather than just one. Then amplify that sound by a factor of 10, and that is just about what we heard as we tried to barrel through the leaves on this trail.

The rest of the ride is less remarkable, as the descending trail loops back to the dirt road. Exposed roots, small logs, and rocks will require you to make technical moves on some portions of the trail. Other sections are smooth and swift. There are some blowdowns near the end of the trail; you will have to carry your bike around them. Once you pop back onto the dirt road, a right turn will lead you on a fast descent back to the starting point.

0.0 Begin by pedaling around the gate across the road.

0.5 There is a four-wheel-drive road on the right; continue straight.

Dirt-road riding is ideal for the whole family, including the dog.

1.5 A single-track trail is to the left; continue straight.

3.5 An old logging road is on the right. Just past this road is a grassy, wide trail. Continue cycling Spencer Branch Road, which makes a hard left turn.

4.2 You will enter a meadow; the dirt road hugs the left side of the meadow. At the far side, turn left onto a grassy, old logging road.

5.2 You will reach a grassy knoll in the trail. The trail continues with a right turn partially obscured by tall grass.

5.5 You will come to a fork in the trail; bear left.

6.5 The trail ends at the intersection with Spencer Branch Road; turn right.

8.2 You will arrive back at the starting point.

Southwest Virginia

Mount Rogers
National Recreation Area

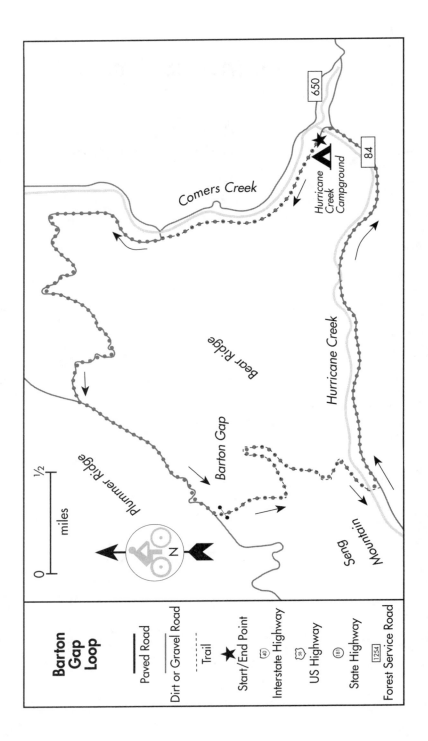

Barton Gap Loop

Paved Road

Dirt or Gravel Road

Trail

★ Start/End Point

🛡 Interstate Highway

🛡 US Highway

🛡 State Highway

1254 Forest Service Road

Comers Creek

Plummer Ridge

Bear Ridge

Barton Gap

Hurricane Creek

Seng Mountain

Hurricane Creek Campground

650

84

½ 0 miles

N

Barton Gap Loop

Distance: 8.3 miles

Difficulty: Moderate

Riding surface: Dirt road, single-track trail

Maps: 1. Mount Rogers National Recreation Area
2. USGS 7.5 minute quadrangle, Troutdale, Va.
3. USGS 7.5 minute quadrangle,
Whitetop Mountain, Va.

Access: From the intersection of U.S. 58 and Va. 91, take U.S. 58 East. Drive 9.5 miles to the intersection with Va. 603. Continue straight on Va. 603 for 10.4 miles to the intersection with Va. 16 in Troutdale. Turn left onto Va. 16. After 2.5 miles, turn left onto F.R. 650 and drive 1.4 miles toward Hurricane Creek Campground. Turn left onto F.R. 84 and drive 0.3 mile. Park at a pull-off on the left.

Elevation change: This ride begins at an elevation of 2,700 feet at the campground. It descends to 2,650 feet at the creek and then climbs to 3,000 feet on the dirt road. The ride drops to 2,800 feet before climbing to 3,200 feet at Barton Gap, then to a maximum of 3,500 feet before it steadily drops back to 2,700 feet at the starting point. The total elevation gain is 1,050 feet.

Configuration: Loop

I t is easy to understand why so many mountain bikers consider Mount Rogers National Recreation Area a mecca, especially when you cycle excellent rides such as this loop.

Barton Gap Loop is a moderately difficult ride due to the endurance it requires, rather than its technical challenge. It begins at Hurricane Creek Campground and soon has you cycling a wide creek-side forest trail. This pretty single-track trail hugging the west bank of Comers Creek is actually an abandoned railroad grade. It follows a gently descending course peppered with annoying rocks. Even if you have front suspension, the rocky surface creates a bumpy ride. Without Rock Shox or other suspension, you'll run a serious risk of having an eyeball or two falling out of socket.

After about a mile, the trail ends at a dirt road. Turn left and cycle uphill, away from the creek. It is a steady climb for about the next 3.5 miles, with a brief respite that lasts only a short half-mile. This dirt road is in good condition, with a smooth, hard-packed surface. During autumn, the leaves of the tall hardwood trees bordering the road are absolutely stunning. When the leaves of trees growing at lower elevations down in the Boone area are just beginning to tease you with a hint of color, these are already at their peak, with glowing golds, reds, and oranges.

The road continues to climb as it passes between Bear Ridge and Plummer Ridge before reaching Barton Gap. You will turn left onto a gated single-track trail that is a shady, pleasant change of pace from the sunny, open dirt road. Though the scenery changes, the climbing continues. After another mile of the low-ring stuff, your prize arrives in the form of a sweet descent laced with some technical sections to test your riding skills. The downhill run is topped off with a watery blast through Hurricane Creek. Just past the creek crossing, a final left turn onto F.R. 84 will lead you down the ridge and back to the campground.

0.0 From the campground gate, cycle downstream to the end of the campground.

0.2 The trail begins on the right at the end of the camp ground.

1.0 You will reach an intersection with F.R. 643. Comers Creek and F.R. 650 are on the right. Turn left onto F.R. 643, a dirt road. Do not cross the creek.

4.3 Turn left onto a gated, old logging road. On the right are an open field and another logging road.

5.8 You will cross Hurricane Creek.

6.0 Turn left onto F.R. 84. This road is open to traffic, so watch out for passing vehicles.

8.3 You will return to the campground entrance and the starting point.

Beautiful single track on the Barton Gap Loop

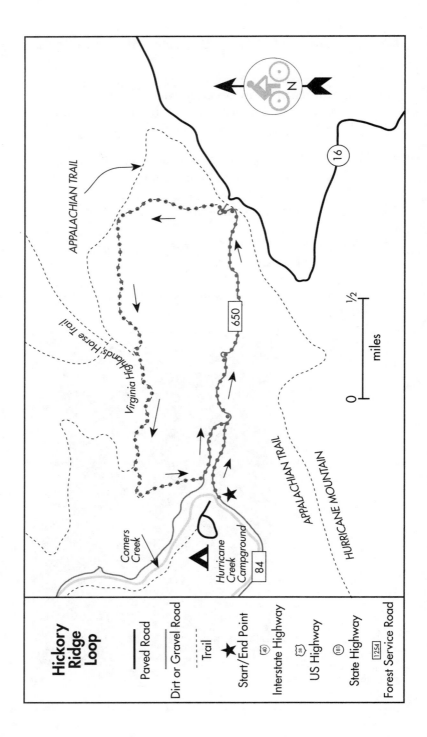

Hickory Ridge Loop

Paved Road

Dirt or Gravel Road

Trail

★ Start/End Point

40 Interstate Highway

58 US Highway

88 State Highway

1254 Forest Service Road

APPALACHIAN TRAIL

Virginia Highlands Horse Trail

Comers Creek

Hurricane Creek Campground

84

650

16

APPALACHIAN TRAIL

HURRICANE MOUNTAIN

N

0   ½
miles

Hickory Ridge Loop

Distance: 5.2 miles

Difficulty: Moderate to strenuous

Riding surface: Dirt road, single-track trail

Maps: 1. Mount Rogers National Recreation Area
2. USGS 7.5 minute quadrangle, Troutdale, Va.

Access: From the intersection of U.S. 58 and Va. 91, take U.S. 58 East. After 9.5 miles, you will reach an intersection with Va. 603. Continue straight on Va. 603 for 10.4 miles to the intersection with Va. 16 in Troutdale. Turn left onto Va. 16. After 2.5 miles, turn left onto F.R. 650 and drive 1.4 miles toward Hurricane Creek Campground. Turn left onto F.R. 84 and drive 0.3 mile. Park at a pull-off on the left.

Elevation change: The ride begins at an elevation of 2,700 feet at the campground. It climbs to 3,300 feet at the turn-off at the Appalachian Trail, then reaches a maximum elevation of 3,600 feet at the top of Hickory Ridge before it begins dropping. The total elevation gain is 900 feet.

Configuration: Loop

Ridge-top riding at its best

Aquick glance at this loop's total distance might make you think this is a cakewalk of a mountain-bike ride. If so, you'd better think again. On one stretch, you'll gain 300 feet in a straight-up grind with no switchbacks to ease the pain. Later, the main descent quickly loses elevation to the tune of 500 feet in about half a mile. We are talking about one tough ride.

The loop begins gently enough on a gradually climbing dirt road. During late fall and winter, when the campground is closed and humans are scarce, you are likely to see some wildlife scampering about the fringes of the road. On one of my rides, I caught a glimpse of a polecat, but it was only fleeting, because he saw me first and skedaddled. White-tailed deer, black bear, and many other animals also live in this neck of the woods.

After warming up on the dirt road, dismount from your mountain bike at the intersection with the Appalachian Trail, turn left, and carry your bike on this white-blazed trail for about a tenth of a mile before turning left onto Hickory Ridge Trail. Mountain bikes are strictly prohibited on the Appalachian Trail; *do not* ride on this brief connector.

Hickory Ridge Trail is a grueling, granny-gear climb to the top of Hickory Ridge; for some, it is a grueling *hike* to the top. Of course, that is because gravity is selective. How else can I explain the fact that I can't make it up some of these hills from hell? Surely, it's not because I'm not strong enough to keep the cranks turning. I've ridden this trail with one macho—maybe even bionic—mountain biker who managed to pedal all the way up, but the rest of our group quickly toppled from lack of forward momentum. We would have been terribly embarrassed by our performance when we finally made the top of the ridge had we not been so preoccupied with trying to breathe.

After the climb comes a pleasant clip along the top of the ridge. This easy section follows a gently descending grade and is spiced with a few logs to play with and jump. In early autumn, this is an especially pretty section, due to the changing foliage of sourwood trees. A harbinger of the coming season, the leaves of sourwoods are some of the first to begin changing color. Turning a deep red, the leaves of the sourwood give us hope that fall is really just around the bend, even though the days are still warm and the forest is still green. Sourwood trees are found throughout the Southeast and are particularly abundant in Great Smoky Mountains National Park. And yes, this is the tree from which delicious sourwood honey is made.

The final drop in this ride is an extremely steep descent best described by the dark smudge of bunched topo lines on the quad map. If the steep grade isn't enough to give you passing thoughts of a shattered clavicle or busted front tooth, then the water bars placed across the trail every hundred feet or so will surely catch your attention. Be extremely cautious. Many a cyclist has performed an ender and subsequent face-plant after hitting these trail obstructions too fast. Though this provides great entertainment for the rest of the cycling party, you probably don't want to return home with granite indentations in your cheeks or, worse yet, shattered bones.

0.0 Begin cycling from the campground entrance.

0.4 You will come to a fork in the road; bear right on F.R. 650.

2.0 Just before reaching Va. 16 (the paved road you drove in on), you will see where the Appalachian Trail crosses F.R. 650. *Stop and dismount.* Turn left onto the Appalachian Trail and *walk* a very short distance on this brief leg of the trail. Mountain bikes are strictly prohibited on the Appalachian Trail; don't even think about riding.

2.1 Turn left onto Hickory Ridge Trail and remount your mountain bike.

Open, sunny trails sure feel good on winter days.

2.7 You will cross the Appalachian Trail and then turn left as the trail swings across the ridge.

3.5 Bear left onto the orange-blazed Virginia Highlands Trail. Watch for horses on this multiuse trail.

4.0 The trail makes a hard left as it descends the mountain.

4.6 Turn left onto F.R. 650.

4.8 Turn right onto F.R. 84 to return to the campground.

5.2 You will arrive back at the starting point.

Exhausted cyclists after Hickory Ridge's climb-from-hell

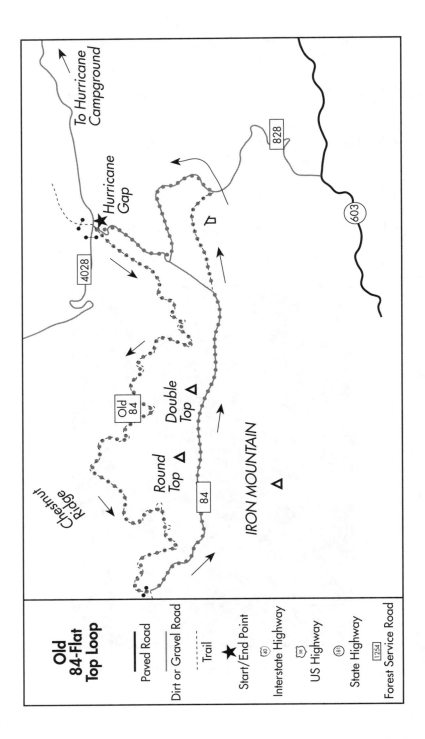

Old 84 - Flat Top Loop

Distance: 10 miles

Difficulty: Moderate

Riding surface: Grassy, old forest-service road, single-track trail, dirt road

Maps: 1. Mount Rogers National Recreation Area
2. USGS 7.5 minute quadrangle, Whitetop Mountain, Va.

Access: From the intersection of U.S. 58 and Va. 91, take U.S. 58 East. Drive 9.5 miles to the intersection with Va. 603. Continue straight on Va. 603 for 10.4 miles to the intersection with Va. 16 in Troutdale. Turn left onto Va. 16 and drive 2.5 miles, then turn left onto F.R. 650 and drive 1.4 miles toward Hurricane Creek Campground. Turn left onto F.R. 84 and drive 3.8 miles to the intersection with Old 84. Bear right on Old 84 and park on the side of the road.

Elevation change: The loop begins at an elevation of 3,800 feet at Hurricane Gap. It slowly creeps up to 4,000 feet near Double Top and then drops back to 3,800 feet at the intersection with F.R. 84. The ride gains 400 painful feet in 0.8 mile on F.R. 84, then an additional 200 feet on Iron Mountain Trail. You will reach the ride's maximum elevation of 4,400 feet by the time you roll past the Cherry Tree Shelter. The total elevation gain is 800 feet.

Configuration: Loop

Pedaling up the grassy double track of Old 84

At the beginning of this loop, you will find yourself pedaling a grassy two-lane track that follows a level grade. The trail weaves back and forth along the side of the mountain and soon begins gaining elevation. The climbing is steady and only mildly difficult for the first 2 miles. At the top of this climb, a meadow filled with tall, tawny grasses borders the trail. A thrilling descent follows which will have you blasting down the grassy double tracks, carving through turns and plunging across small streams that dare to cross your path.

This section of the ride is spiced with a few more climbs and descents before the grassy road spills onto F.R. 84, a hard-packed dirt road. Though you will want to turn right to avoid the hill looming over your shoulder, you must turn left to continue this loop. Click into your granny gear and keep those cranks turning; this strenuous pull lasts for less than a mile. If you can lift your eyes from your slowly turning front wheel, there is a beautiful view on the left about halfway up the hill.

A swift descent to the turnoff for Iron Mountain Trail follows. This yellow-blazed path will soon have you scratching up the side of a bony, technical section of single-track trail. At the top of the ridge is the Cherry Tree Shelter, which makes a great place to stop and rest and replace those spent carbos with some sports bars. It's mostly downhill from here.

Thanks to the shade from a mature deciduous forest, this loop makes a great summertime ride. The trail is also wide enough to keep irritating, grabby undergrowth from creeping in too close and stinging and slapping your legs. Most mountain bikers love tight single-track trails but hate those narrow paths in the dead of summer, when blackberry bushes and briers threaten to take back the trail. It's no fun to blast down a trail only to have prickly flora slicing your legs, drawing blood, and leaving thorns in your calves as take-home party favors.

0.0 Begin cycling on the first dirt road on the left. You will have to cross a dirt barrier immediately. Do not begin on the gated road just past this first road; do not begin on the horse trail.

Pausing for a rest at the Cherry Tree Shelter

0.8 There are two berms, or "tank traps," across the trail. This grassy road continues on a moderately ascending grade.

1.9 A clearing is on the left; continue straight on a descending grade.

4.8 A field is on the right. Just past this field is a gate across the path. Cycle around the gate to continue.

4.9 Turn left onto F.R. 84 and get ready to click into your granny gear for the tough climb ahead.

5.4 There is a nice view to the left.

5.6 You will reach the end of the climb. Hallelujah!

6.7 Turn right off F.R. 84 onto a newly cut logging road.

6.8 Cycle around the gate across the road. Prepare to climb for the next 0.5 mile on the yellow-blazed Iron Mountain Trail.

7.9 The Cherry Tree Shelter is on the right. Continue straight on what is now a blue-blazed descending trail. (Note: To shorten the ride a bit, you can turn left onto Iron Mountain Trail to continue; this trail spills onto F.R. 828 above the climb described below.)

8.2 Cycle around the gate across the trail. Turn left onto F.R. 828 and climb on this red-clay road for several tenths of a mile.

9.2 F.R. 828 intersects F.R. 84. Turn right onto F.R. 84 for a final, fast descent. Yee-ha!

10.0 You will arrive back at the starting point.

Taking a break in a warm sunny meadow

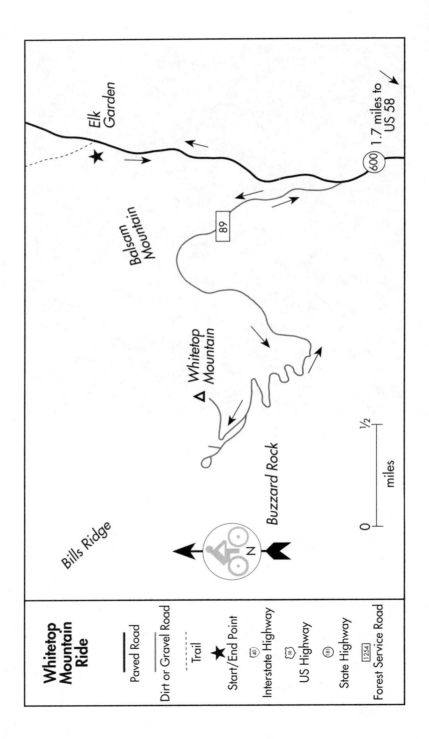

Whitetop Mountain Ride

Paved Road

Dirt or Gravel Road

Trail

★ Start/End Point

Interstate Highway

US Highway

State Highway

Forest Service Road

Elk Garden

Balsam Mountain

Whitetop Mountain

Bills Ridge

Buzzard Rock

89

600 1.7 miles to US 58

N

0   ½
miles

Whitetop Mountain Ride

Distance: 8.4 miles

Difficulty: Moderate

Riding surface: Dirt road, paved road

Maps: 1. Mount Rogers National Recreation Area
2. USGS 7.5 minute quadrangle, Whitetop Mountain, Va.

Access: From the intersection of U.S. 58 and Va. 91, take U.S. 58 East. Drive 9.5 miles to the intersection with Va. 603. Turn right to stay on U.S. 58. Drive 7.7 miles to the intersection with F.R. 600. Turn left onto this paved road. Drive 2.7 miles (past the F.R. 89 turnoff to Whitetop Mountain) and park at the large parking lot on the left at Elk Garden. There is a pay telephone located in this parking lot.

Elevation change: The ride begins at an elevation of 4,500 feet at Elk Garden. There is a slight elevation gain on F.R. 600, but the serious ascent begins on F.R. 89; you will reach an elevation of about 5,000 feet in the first few miles. A final gain is tallied on the switchbacks to the top of the mountain. At the summit of Whitetop Mountain, you will reach a maximum elevation of about 5,500 feet. The total elevation gain is 1,000 feet.

Configuration: Out-and-back

Snow-crusted summit of Whitetop Mountain

This is a moderately difficult ride which begins on a paved forest-service road, F.R. 600. This road is flanked by a mixed hardwood forest and has a relatively easy grade. A right turn on F.R. 89 will start you on a gradual climb toward the peak of Whitetop Mountain. This dirt road cuts a fairly straightforward path up the mountain between walls of tall, slender hardwood trees. You will enjoy a brief reprieve from the climb after less than a mile on this road, though the climbing continues with a vengeance about half a mile later.

When you reach the switchbacks in the road (and the 5,000-foot elevation line), you will find that the scenery changes dramatically. Rather than cycling through a heavily forested area, you will find yourself pedaling across an open bald. The vastness is occasionally interrupted by a shock of evergreens permanently bent and contorted by blustery winds, snow, and ice. It is certainly no mystery why the mountain was named Whitetop. Judging from an early-October ride of mine, when the bald was already coated with sparkling frost and ice, this tundra is no stranger to the frozen stuff. Local folks say you can expect to find the top of this mountain snow- or ice-covered as late as the month of May. So even though you may be comfortable down in the valley wearing bicycling shorts and a T-shirt, be prepared with long-fingered gloves, a jacket, and tights to ward off the cold temperatures and colder gusts of wind teasing Whitetop's summit.

Near the top of the mountain, the road is littered with rocks and potholes. Though the ride is not technical, these obstructions will require that you pick a line to avoid tweaking a tire and crashing. Panoramic views of Buzzard Rock, Beech Mountain, and other surrounding mountains of Virginia, Tennessee, and North Carolina are sure to make the climbing worthwhile.

0.0 From the parking lot at Elk Garden, cycle south on F.R. 600, a paved road.

1.2 Turn right onto F.R. 89, a dirt road. You will continue a gradual climb.

1.9 The grade of the road levels out.

2.5 The road begins climbing again.

3.8 There is a fork in the road; bear left.

3.9 There is another fork in the road; bear left again. If you bear right, the road will take you to an electrical tower on top of the mountain.

4.0 Bear left at the fork in the road.

4.2 At the top of the mountain, turn around and begin retracing your path. It's all downhill from here. Enjoy the descent. You've earned it!

8.4 You will arrive back at the starting point at Elk Garden.

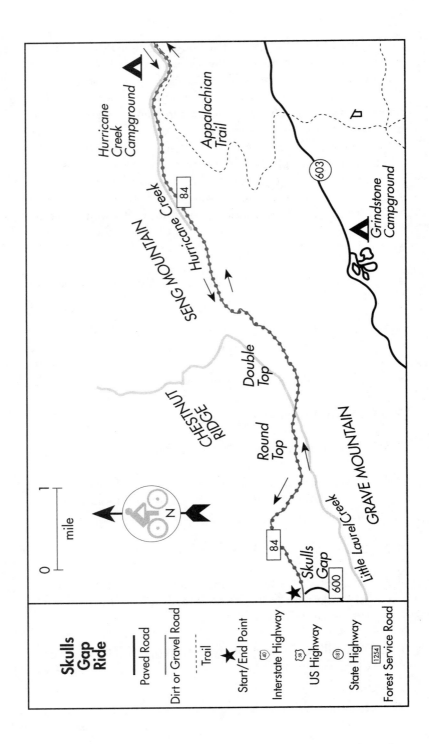

Skulls Gap Ride

Paved Road

Dirt or Gravel Road

Trail

★ Start/End Point

㊵ Interstate Highway

🄺 US Highway

⑱ State Highway

1254 Forest Service Road

N

0 1

mile

Hurricane Creek Campground

Appalachian Trail

Grindstone Campground

603

SENG MOUNTAIN

Hurricane Creek

84

CHESTNUT RIDGE

Double Top

Round Top

GRAVE MOUNTAIN

Little Laurel Creek

84

Skulls Gap

600

Skulls Gap Ride

Distance: 17.8 miles

Difficulty: Strenuous

Riding surface: Dirt road

Maps: 1. Mount Rogers National Recreation Area
2. USGS 7.5 minute quadrangle, Whitetop Mountain, Va.
3. USGS 7.5 minute quadrangle, Troutdale, Va.

Access: From the intersection of U.S. 58 and Va. 91, take U.S. 58 East. Drive 9.5 miles to the intersection with Va. 603. Continue straight on Va. 603 until you reach the intersection with Va. 600. Turn left onto Va. 600 and drive 2.7 miles to Skulls Gap Picnic Area. Park here.

Elevation change: From the 3,500-foot elevation at Skulls Gap, the ride begins with a descent to 3,400 feet before rising back to 3,500 feet. It then rises steadily to a maximum elevation of 4,200 feet near Double Top Mountain. A descent to the minimum elevation of 2,700 feet along Hurricane Creek at the campground follows. You will then turn around and retrace your path to the starting point at Skulls Gap. The total round-trip elevation gain is 2,400 feet.

Configuration: Out-and-back

Equestrians enjoy the trails of Mount Rogers National Recreation Area as much as mountain bikers.

Kristi Spears Jennings, a good friend of mine, is renowned in our bicycling club for chanting "Hills are my friends, hills are my friends" on climbs. They must be her friends, because in 1988 she set a record for the fastest time by a female in the Assault on Mount Mitchell bike race. And that course offers some of the most brutal climbing in the Southeast!

As I struggled up the challenging ascents on this ride, I thought of Kristi and her hill theory quite a bit. I muttered the chant a few times but finally gave up. These hills seem anything but friendly.

This is a formidable ride softened only by blessed downhills and pristine wilderness surroundings. The road winds up and down the hills of Iron Mountain as it leaves Skulls Gap in pursuit of Hurricane Gap. High ridge-top sections offer beautiful views of nearby mountains and distant towns nestled in the valley. The scenery varies from gray hardwood trunks adorned with green, leafy tresses in summer to the verdant creek-side flora that colors the landscape year-round. It is along these damp banks that glossy-leaved rhododendron bushes mingle with the lacy fringes of hemlock trees. An early-summer ride is certain to make you catch your breath when you round the first bend near Hurricane Creek and are bombarded with the stunning sight and the fragrant scent of pink rhododendron blossoms.

The ride is not technically challenging, but there are rough and rocky stretches of road that will require you to carefully pick a line. This out-and-back route will lead you to dry ridge lines high in the hills and drop you down beside picturesque mountain creeks. It will give you just about all you could ask for from a physical workout in perhaps the most beautiful natural gym around.

0.0 The ride begins at Skulls Gap on F.R. 84, a wide dirt road. You will come to a fork in the road almost immediately; bear right.

0.4 There is a parking pull-off on the right; continue straight. A creek is on the left side of the road.

1.5 You will reach a Y-intersection; F.R. 84 bears right. There is a gated road on the left with a sign saying that it is closed to all motor vehicles. You will begin a moderate climb just past this intersection.

4.4 On the right is F.R. 828, a dirt road. You will be descending at this point.

5.0 An unmarked dirt road bleeds into F.R. 84. Continue straight.

6.8 A hiking trail is on the right. On the left is one of the trails described in the Barton Gap Loop chapter of this book.

7.5 An unmarked single-track trail is on the left.

8.6 On the left is a dirt road with a wooden gate; this road is closed to traffic. Continue straight.

8.9 You will arrive at a stop sign near the entrance to Hurricane Creek Campground. Turn around and begin retracing your path. (Note: You can cut this ride in half and eliminate the toughest climb by leaving a vehicle at the campground and setting up a shuttle.)

17.8 You will arrive back at the starting point at Skulls Gap. Wouldn't an oxygen mask be nice right about now?

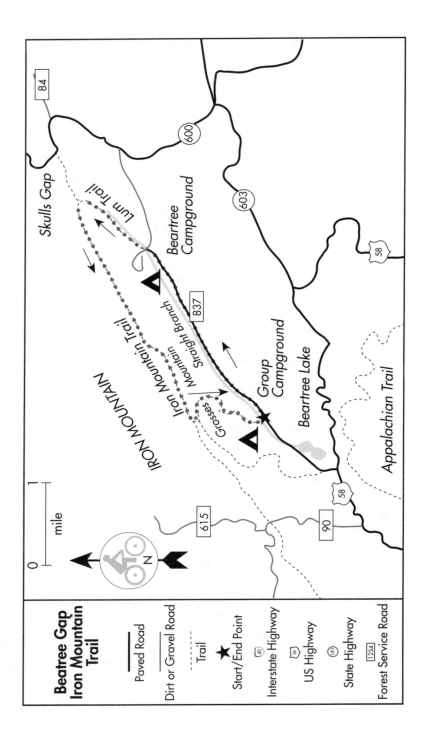

Beartree Gap / Iron Mountain Trail Loop

Distance: 8 miles

Difficulty: Moderate

Riding surface: Single-track trail, paved road

Maps: 1. Mount Rogers National Recreation Area
2. USGS 7.5 minute quadrangle, Konnarock, Va.

Access: From the intersection of U.S. 58 and Va. 91, take U.S. 58 East. After 7.5 miles, turn left onto Beartree Gap Road (F.R. 837). Drive 1.5 miles to Beartree Group Campground, on the left. Park at any pull-off near the entrance of the campground, making sure you do not block the gate if it is closed. To avoid the $3 parking fee, you can park in the fisherman's parking lot near the fee station.

Elevation change: The ride begins at an elevation of 3,000 feet and climbs to 3,300 feet at the entrance to Beartree Recreation Area. It gains another 500 feet on Lum Trail, reaching 3,800 feet at the intersection with Iron Mountain Trail. The ride reaches a maximum elevation of 3,950 feet on Iron Mountain Trail before it drops back to 3,800 feet. The elevation quickly drops on the descent across Grosses Mountain. The total elevation gain is 950 feet.

Configuration: Loop

Taking a breather on the Iron Mountain Trail

I am beginning to tire of superlatives like *outstanding, exciting,* and *beautiful.* However, when it comes to describing trails in Mount Rogers National Recreation Area, these words just seem to gush from my pen. This ride, offering moderately difficult challenges, exciting descents, and beautiful surroundings, is so popular that a local mountain-biking club uses it as a course for competitive races.

The ride begins on Beartree Gap Road, a paved road which offers a good warmup as it gently climbs toward Beartree Recreation Area. The natural beauty of the forest flanking the road is highlighted by the trickling waters of Straight Branch Creek, located on the north side of the road. You will have a closer view of this pretty mountain stream when you begin cycling the first single-track trail of this loop, Lum Trail.

Once on Lum Trail, you will have a chance to exercise your technical prowess. The trail is strewn with rocks and downed tree limbs, which will keep you on your toes. Though it begins as a wide single track with plenty of maneuvering room, it squeezes down to a very narrow path which makes for a tight fit for you and your mountain bike. The grade is level at the beginning of the trail but steepens to a strenuous climb on the approach to Iron Mountain Trail. If you are exhausted by the time you reach the trail shelter located on the left side of Lum Trail, then you're in trouble, because the real climbing is about to begin.

A left turn onto the yellow-blazed Iron Mountain Trail will find you on a narrow trail surrounded by a mature hardwood forest. For about the first mile and a half, you will encounter several sections that are quite strenuous and technical. Thankfully, the difficulty eventually eases, giving you a welcome opportunity to let your heart rate drop—to maybe 180 beats a minute or so. You might even appreciate a look at the beautiful woodland scenery enveloping the trail. Up until now, you probably weren't too interested in sightseeing. It's hard to ooh and aah when all your energy is being spent trying to move your bike up what seems like Mount Everest.

An October mountain-bike ride is especially pretty. If you keep your eyes to the ground, you may see the yellow of fallen birch leaves, a sharp contrast against the dark soil of the trail. The leaves look like shiny gold medallions scattered across black velvet. On one such ride, I almost got the feeling that I had interrupted bartering between early white settlers and Indians. I half-expected to glimpse Indians quietly slipping from the safe cover of the woods when I turned around to look back down the trail.

Though the trail has a few more dips and climbs, it maintains a near-constant elevation of 3,800 feet as it cuts a westward swath across the southern side of Iron Mountain. You will encounter a gentle descent before reaching the intersection at Shaw Gap. At this saddle in Iron Mountain, a left turn will take you on a fast, fun descent that begins on an unmarked, wide single-track trail. As the trail slices across Grosses Mountain on its way down to the campground, it narrows and becomes very technical. There are some grassy sections that will spit you through tight tunnels of mountain laurel, creating a wildly sensational descent. Then, just before the campground, the trail blows out of the dense forest and lands in an open meadow. Even though you are almost at the end of the ride,

The shelter on the Iron Mountain Trail makes a good resting spot.

you might not be able to resist the temptation to stop and rest in this clearing. If you don't watch yourself, the warm sunshine will sedate you and leave you sprawling in the grass, half-asleep, like an old yard dog.

0.0 Begin at the pull-off near the entrance to Beartree Group Campground. Cycle up the paved Beartree Gap Road toward the main campground.

2.5 You will reach a traffic circle at the campground entrance; turn left. Continue straight past Straight Branch Trail, on the right.

2.6 Turn right onto Lum Trail. The trailhead is a bit hidden; it is located just behind the restrooms.

3.5 You will pass a trail shelter on the left.

3.6 You will reach the intersection of Lum Trail and Iron Mountain Trail. Turn left onto the yellow-blazed Iron Mountain Trail.

6.7 You will reach an intersection of unmarked trails; turn left.

6.8 You will reach a T-intersection of unmarked trails; turn left again.

8.0 You will arrive back at the starting point at Beartree Group Campground. Wasn't that a great ride?

Wimping out on a technical section of trail

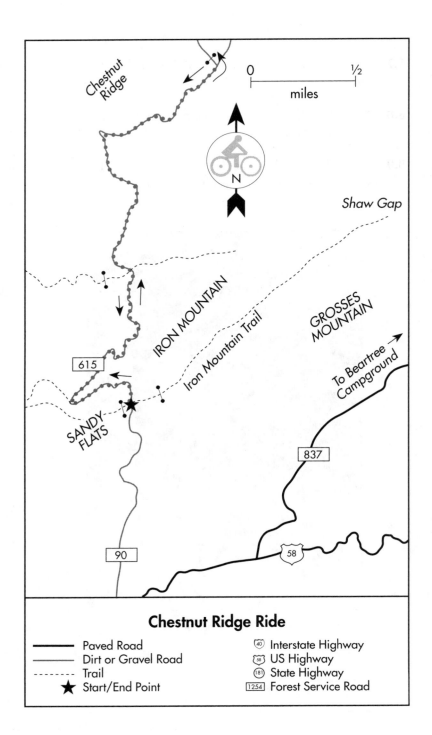

Chestnut Ridge

Shaw Gap

IRON MOUNTAIN

GROSSES MOUNTAIN

Iron Mountain Trail

To Beartree Campground

615

SANDY FLATS

837

90

58

0   ½
miles

N

Chestnut Ridge Ride

—— Paved Road

—— Dirt or Gravel Road

- - - - Trail

★ Start/End Point

(40) Interstate Highway

(58) US Highway

(181) State Highway

1254 Forest Service Road

Chestnut Ridge Ride

Distance: 7.6 miles

Difficulty: Moderate

Riding surface: Dirt road

Maps: 1. Mount Rogers National Recreation Area
2. USGS 7.5 minute quadrangle, Konnarock, Va.

Access: From the intersection of U.S. 58 and Va. 91, take U.S. 58 East. Drive approximately 6 miles to the intersection with F.R. 90. Turn left onto F.R. 90 and drive 1.4 miles to a small, unpaved parking area at the top of the hill.

Elevation change: The ride begins at an elevation of 3,400 feet on F.R. 90. On F.R. 615, it drops several hundred feet in the first mile. A near-constant elevation of 3,000 feet is maintained for a mile or so along the banks of Rush Creek before a final drop to 2,700 feet along the southern border of Chestnut Ridge. The climb back up is steady and fairly gentle until the final push to the F.R. 90 turnoff. The total elevation gain is 700 feet.

Configuration: Out-and-back

A long the northern slope of Iron Mountain lies a beautiful stretch of dirt road begging for the knobby tires of mountain bikes. The gurgle of sparkling mountain streams and the call of a red-tailed hawk might be the only sounds you hear in these remote woods. Except for the occasional openings through the trees giving glimpses of

Beautiful views abound in Mount Rogers National Recreation Area.

distant towns, you could easily imagine yourself deep in the heart of the wilderness, miles from civilization. Thick grapevines wind through some of the trees, seductively draping their branches. Some of the hemlocks and hardwoods are so huge that they are reminiscent of virgin stands like those of Joyce Kilmer Memorial Forest. Though this is not virgin forest, it is obvious that loggers haven't been in this neck of the woods for quite some time.

The ride begins on a narrow, gently descending road that ultimately passes along the southern border of Chestnut Ridge. Rather than bursting through the woods in a straight-line shot, the road carves a meandering path through incredibly beautiful forest. These dense woods are filled with typical Appalachian flora: hemlock, pine, rhododendron, mixed hardwoods, and, at the higher elevations, mountain laurel. Because of this mix of conifers and deciduous trees, you can expect to be enveloped by a verdant forest all seasons of the year. Though we tend to think of autumn as the most sensational season for colors, late spring offers its own splendor. As the hardwoods leaf out, species by species and week by week, the forest seems to explode into a thousand shades of green.

It's true that this route offers no single track, but that doesn't mean it is technically unchallenging. There are rough sections along the way that will have you weaving from one side of the road to the other in order to pedal the path of least resistance. Other sections, smooth and groomed, offer a respite from picking and choosing the most unobstructed line. The descents are mostly gentle and relaxing, offering ample opportunity to appreciate the surrounding beauty while spinning down the road. But there are a few deliciously steep downhills thrown in that will have the forest whipping past in a blur and the air stinging your cheeks.

The return trip poses some climbing, but nothing serious until you near the intersection with F.R. 90.

0.0   The ride begins on F.R. 90, a dirt road.

0.4   You will arrive at an intersection of dirt roads and trails. Make a hard right turn onto F.R. 615.

0.8   The road makes a sharp right turn.

1.3   You will see a small creek trickling through the woods on the left side of the road.

1.5   The road bends to the right. You will notice a gated road to the left and a fence on the edge of a boggy clearing. Just past this area is a narrow single-track trail on the right. Continue pedaling the main dirt road, F.R. 615.

2.1   The road slices through an extremely rocky section of forest.

2.7   There is a beautiful view on the left.

3.8   Private roads are on the left and right. The road continues, but the scenic natural areas do not. Turn around here and retrace your path to the starting point.

7.6   You will arrive back at the starting point on F.R. 90.

Note: Because these roads are ungated, you should exercise caution, as if a vehicle is just around the next bend. However, it is unlikely that you will see any motorists.

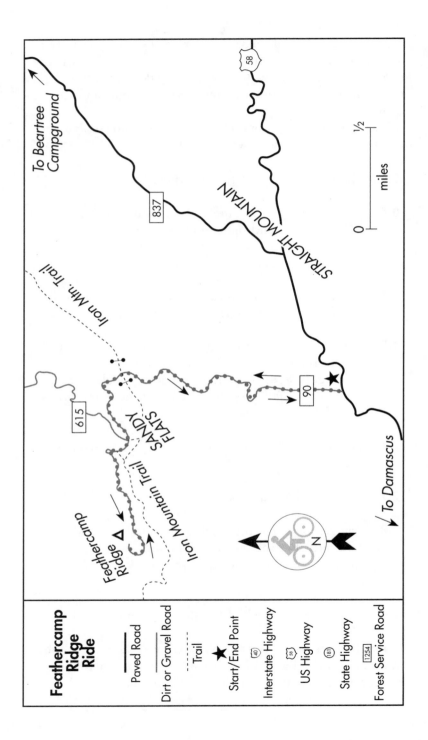

Feathercamp Ridge Ride

Paved Road
Dirt or Gravel Road
Trail
★ Start/End Point
🟤 Interstate Highway
🛡 US Highway
⬡ State Highway
1254 Forest Service Road

To Beartree Campground

837

58

STRAIGHT MOUNTAIN

0 ½
miles

Iron Mtn. Trail

615

SANDY FLATS

Feathercamp Ridge △

Iron Mountain Trail

90

To Damascus

N

Feathercamp Ridge Ride

Distance: 5.4 miles

Difficulty: Moderate

Riding surface: Dirt road

Maps: 1. Mount Rogers National Recreation Area
2. USGS 7.5 minute quadrangle, Konnarock, Va.

Access: From the intersection of U.S. 58 and Va. 91, take U.S. 58 East. Drive approximately 6 miles to the intersection with F.R. 90. Turn left onto F.R. 90 and park at any nearby pull-off.

Elevation change: The ride begins at an elevation of 2,800 feet and quickly climbs to 3,400 feet in the first mile. The elevation remains constant through Sandy Flats. The climbing resumes on the stretch of road leading up to the former site of the Feathercamp Lookout Tower. The maximum elevation is 3,750 feet. It is all downhill back to the starting point. The total elevation gain is 950 feet.

Configuration: Out-and-back

Gorgeous, natural scenery highlights this dirt road.

This is an ideal ride if you are short on daylight and want to get in a good workout before the sun drops from the sky and disappears in the dark shadows of the mountains. It follows a hard-packed-dirt forest-service road as it slices across Iron Mountain and climbs to the top of Feathercamp Ridge. Most of the ride is unchallenging from a technical standpoint, though there is a fairly technical section of road between Sandy Flats and the ridge top.

Loggers have cleared some sections of forest along the road, creating outstanding views of Whitetop Mountain and Mount Rogers, this area's namesake. From this vantage, the flat, bald summit of Whitetop Mountain appears to loom higher than the hogback shape of Mount Rogers, but in fact, Mount Rogers is king at 5,729 feet, while Whitetop Mountain comes in at 5,344 feet. There are more views of other mountains as you grind to the top of Feathercamp Ridge, but if you are anything like my friends and me, you won't be too interested in the scenery by this point in the ride. We were far more interested in getting to the top and pointing our handlebars downhill.

It's a madman descent, with some sections rough and technical, some smooth and sweet. You'll be "spitting out" elevation like a child spits out black jellybeans. The road swings around tight turns that will have you kicking up dirt and sticks along the shoulders and rubbing elbows with the dense rhododendron thickets. Where the road drops into shady mountain gaps, you'll find that the temperature, at least in winter, drops almost as quickly as the elevation. During cold weather, you might want to pull on your jacket before you take the plunge down these hills. You definitely will not want to interrupt the fun by having to stop halfway down for a warm-clothing pit stop.

0.0 Begin cycling at the pull-off on F.R. 90.

0.5 There is a good view of Whitetop Mountain on the right.

0.6 A gated road is on the left; continue straight.

1.0 A gated logging road forks off F.R. 90; continue straight.

1.4 You will arrive at a small parking area. Iron Mountain Trail crosses F.R. 90 at this point.

1.8 You will arrive at an intersection of dirt roads and trails; continue on F.R. 90 by bearing slightly to the right.

1.9 A single-track trail is on the left; continue straight.

2.0 A gated logging road is on the right; bear left to continue.

2.7 You will arrive at the former site of the Feathercamp Lookout Tower. Turn around and retrace your path to the starting point. It's a piece of cake all the way back.

5.4 You will reach the starting point and the end of the ride.

Note: This dirt road is not gated and therefore is open to vehicles. Though traffic is light, you should be very cautious on the turns, particularly on the descent.

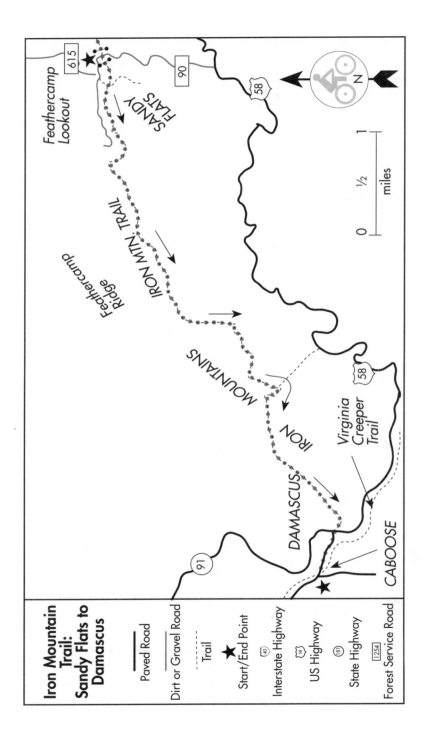

Iron Mountain Trail: Sandy Flats to Damascus

Paved Road

Dirt or Gravel Road

Trail

★ Start/End Point

⬡ Interstate Highway

⬡ US Highway

⬡ State Highway

▭ Forest Service Road

Feathercamp Lookout

SANDY FLATS

IRON MTN TRAIL

Feathercamp Ridge

IRON MOUNTAINS

Virginia Creeper Trail

DAMASCUS

CABOOSE

N

0   ½   1
miles

615

90

58

58

91

Iron Mountain Trail: Sandy Flats to Damascus

Distance: 6.4 miles

Difficulty: Moderate

Riding surface: Single-track trail, dirt road

Maps: 1. Mount Rogers National Recreation Area
2. USGS 7.5 minute quadrangle, Konnarock, Va.
3. USGS 7.5 minute quadrangle, Damascus, Va.

Access: To reach the Sandy Flats access, take U.S. 58 East from the intersection of U.S. 58 and Va. 91. Drive approximately 6 miles to the intersection with F.R. 90. Turn left onto F.R. 90 and drive 1.4 miles to the small pull-off near Sandy Flats.

To reach the Damascus access, take U.S. 58 West from the intersection of U.S. 58 and Va. 91. Drive through the town of Damascus for 1.5 miles to the red caboose at the Virginia Creeper trailhead. Park in this parking area.

Note: U.S. 58 makes several turns through Damascus; just follow the highway signs and make the appropriate turns.

Elevation change: The ride begins at an elevation of about 3,400 feet at Sandy Flats. On Iron Mountain Trail, there is a gentle climb to about 3,500 feet. The elevation remains constant for a mile or so before a steady descent to 2,900 feet at the turnoff onto the old Appalachian Trail. Though the topographical lines indicate only a descent along the trail, there are a few buckles that require some brief, easy climbing. The elevation drops quickly as the trail shoots for home. The ride reaches 1,950 feet when it hits pavement at the U.S. 58 intersection. The total elevation gain is only about 100 feet.

Configuration: One-way

It's a tight fit, but that just makes it more fun!

Pedaling at a brisk speed down this black trail snaking through the woods, all you are likely to see is a green and gray kaleidoscope image of leaves and trunks rushing by. Azure Virginia skies occasionally pop into view but are quickly obscured by the dense canopy of foliage hovering overhead.

Though this trail winds through a beautiful hardwood forest, the near-constant descending grade doesn't allow much opportunity for sightseeing. But with all the braking action, you will eventually have to stop to rest your strained hand muscles for a minute or two. And when you do, be sure to cast an eye to the woods, where you will see a dense forest filled with typical Appalachian vegetation. Mountain laurel, hemlock, pine, dogwood, poplar, and white oak are some of the many trees that enclose this narrow trail. Rhododendron and other moisture-loving flora abound along the creeks and streams toward the lower end of the trail.

There are some sections of this undulating terrain that will get you up on your pedals, but most of the ride traces descending ridge lines. Some of the descents are fast and smooth, while others slow you down with their rocky, technical twists.

The final drop into Damascus is along the old Appalachian Trail. This last mile follows a very technical descending line through the woods. A number of creeks and streams thread their way across the trail. The streambeds are especially rocky and obstructed, posing a real challenge to mountain bikers insistent on pedaling through them.

This portion of Iron Mountain Trail is no longer marked with bright yellow blazes, as the trail was through the upper miles. You will need to follow the faded white blazes which once faithfully guided tired, blistered Appalachian Trail hikers. You will see the freshly painted white blazes of the newly rerouted Appalachian Trail, but remember that mountain bikes are strictly prohibited on this legendary hiking trail.

0.0 After leaving a shuttle vehicle at the caboose in Damascus, begin cycling up F.R. 90 from the pull-off at Sandy Flats.

0.4 You will arrive at an intersection of dirt roads and trails; remain on F.R. 90 by continuing straight and bearing slightly to the right. (A hard right turn will put you on F.R. 615.)

0.5 Iron Mountain Trail is on the left. Turn onto this narrow single-track trail marked with yellow blazes.

1.4 You will arrive at an intersection of trails; bear left to continue on Iron Mountain Trail. There is a large oak tree with a yellow blaze at this trail junction.

3.1 Iron Mountain Trail spills out onto a dirt road. Turn left and descend on this newly cut logging road. There are yellow blazes on some of the roadside trees to guide you.

Despite being high in the hills, there are still some level spots on the trails in Mount Rogers National Recreation Area.

3.4   Leave the logging road and turn left to return to single-track trail. This is a tricky turn, so be on the lookout for it. The trail, a narrow single track marked with a yellow blaze, is located on the left at a bend in road. Just past the turnoff, the road bends to the right and begins a climb.

4.3   You will arrive at the intersection of Iron Mountain Trail and the Appalachian Trail. There is a large tree painted with a yellow arrow pointing to the right. Turn right to continue on Iron Mountain Trail. The yellow blazes end at this point. This is the old Appalachian Trail, so you will see faded white blazes on some of the trees; the rerouted Appalachian Trail has fresh, obvious white blazes.

5.5   The trail ends at a dirt road. Continue pedaling straight onto this dirt road. You will pass through a neighborhood of houses. Be prepared to be chased by a dog or two.

5.9 You will reach U.S. 58 in front of Cowboy's convenience store. Turn right to return to the caboose.

6.4 You will return to the starting point at the Virginia Creeper trailhead.

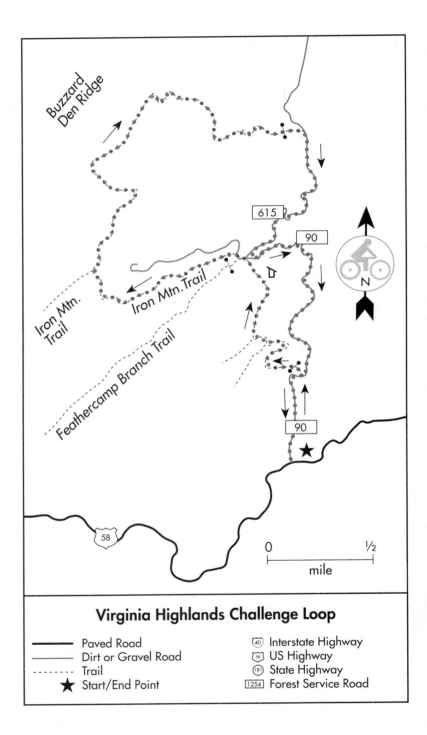

Buzzard
Den Ridge

615

90

Iron Mtn.
Trail

Iron Mtn. Trail

Feathercamp Branch Trail

90

N

58

0   ½
mile

Virginia Highlands Challenge Loop

——— Paved Road
——— Dirt or Gravel Road
- - - - Trail
★ Start/End Point

40 Interstate Highway
58 US Highway
18 State Highway
1254 Forest Service Road

Virginia Highlands Challenge Loop

Distance: 8 miles

Difficulty: Moderate to strenuous

Riding surface: Single-track trail, dirt roads, gravel roads

Maps: 1. Mount Rogers National Recreation Area
2. USGS 7.5 minute quadrangle, Konnarock, Va.

Access: From the intersection of U.S. 58 and Va. 91, take U.S. 58 East. Drive approximately 6 miles to the intersection with F.R. 90. Turn left onto F.R. 90 and park at a pull-off on the right.

Elevation change: The loop begins at an elevation of about 2,900 feet on F.R. 90. It climbs steadily to 3,100 feet at the first turnoff. You will gain another 400 feet on this grassy, old logging road and short, steep single-track trail connector, reaching a maximum of 3,500 feet. A descent to F.R. 90 follows. You will do more climbing on Iron Mountain Trail, to the tune of about 150 feet of elevation. A final, steady climb on F.R. 615 adds another 350 feet. A short ascent on F.R. 90 tops the ride off with 50 final feet before a swift, sweet descent back to 2,900 feet at the starting point. The total elevation gain is 1,150 feet.

Configuration: Loop

Virginia trails seem custom-made for mountain bikes.

One of the great features of mountain biking is the surprise element. It's that promise of adventure. It's discovering new paths while cycling a tried-and-true route. And when you do, it's like finding money on the street.

You know what I mean. A buddy tells you about a good ride, tells you where to go, tells you what to expect. And then while you're out pedaling your friend's ride, you happen to notice a half-hidden, inviting green tunnel of single track seductively curling into the forest. Hitting your brakes, you twirl around in a cloud of flying gravel, dirt, and sticks to be sure it isn't a mirage. No, it's real. So it's off the gravel road and onto the trail for some reconnaissance pedaling.

Many times, these delicious diversions look promising, only to peter out into nothing more than a tangled wall of briers and underbrush. But once in a while, you find a trail that becomes your favorite ride, your personal find, your private Elysium.

That's just about what happened to me when a few of my friends and I set out to pedal a route that Byrum Geisler of Abingdon recommended. We were driving up to the trailhead when I noticed a gated logging road flagged with a fluorescent orange arrow. My gaze locked on the path as our car continued up the dirt road. Hmm, this looked interesting. A trail with such obvious potential for mountain biking just couldn't be passed up, now could it? "Stop the car!" I screeched. Groans and moans poured from the car as my so-called friends began dredging up stories of past explorations that had failed. But they reluctantly agreed to give it a try. As we sized up the loop possibilities, notes and papers and maps tumbled back and forth from front seat to back like laundry in a dryer. Finally, we shoved off.

To make a long story short, we had come upon the race loop for the Virginia Highlands Mountain Bicycle Club's 1994 Mountain Bike Challenge. Members of the club had worked feverishly to clear trails of downed trees and debris in time for their May Day race. The results were amazing. These folks had obviously invested considerable time, energy, and elbow grease in the project. The single-track portions of the loop were as smooth as a baby's behind. All of the route was virtually free from obstructions, creating one of the best mountain-bike rides in Mount Rogers.

The loop is an invigorating combination of grassy logging roads, narrow single-track trails, and climbing gravel roads. The climbing sections are sandwiched between intermittent down-hills, tempering the overall severity of the ride. Some of these downhills are gentle enough to give you a chance to catch your breath. But others don't give you much time to relax. Some of these paths follow tight, technical single-track trails that dangle on the edge of steep ridges. As your wheels tiptoe down the only line possible, you realize that there isn't much of a margin for error. Others are near-vertical descents that bottom out in streams filled with slippery, moss-covered stones.

This ride gives cyclists challenges and thrills galore, and even throws in some pretty views for good measure.

0.0   Begin cycling from the pull-off on F.R. 90, a climbing dirt road.

0.5   There is a good view of Whitetop Mountain on the right.

0.6   A gated, old logging road is on the left; turn onto this climbing, grassy road.

1.0   There is a narrow single-track trail on the right that climbs straight up the ridge. Turn onto this trail. A big hickory tree and a stream are on the right at this turnoff. You will have to dismount and carry your bike for about 25 yards up the steep trail. (In case you miss the trail, note that the logging road begins descending just past the turnoff.)

1.1 The steep trail ends at an intersection with a wide trail. Turn right onto the wide trail and get back on your bike.

1.6 You will arrive at an intersection of trails. Steps are built into the trail on the right; a picnic table and shelter are on the left. Continue the loop by going straight on the descending trail.

1.7 The trail spills onto F.R. 90. The gated Feathercamp Trail is on the left; F.R. 615 bears right. Turn left and follow F.R. 90 as it climbs toward Iron Mountain Trail.

Pedaling up the gravel road of F. R. 615

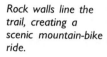
Rock walls line the trail, creating a scenic mountain-bike ride.

1.8 Turn left onto the yellow-blazed Iron Mountain Trail, a narrow single-track trail seen easily from the road.

1.9 There is a single-track trail on the left leading to Sandy Flats; continue straight.

2.8 You will arrive at an intersection of trails; bear right to continue the loop. Iron Mountain Trail turns left here at the large oak tree marked with a yellow blaze; do not take it.

3.4 You will bear to the right and climb briefly.

3.5 You will make a hard left turn onto a level four-wheel-drive road.

4.0 There is a beautiful view on the left.

4.1 You will reach a tricky, dangerous descent; exercise caution.

4.7 The trail enters a meadow; continue straight.

5.0 You will pedal around a gate in the trail. Turn right onto F.R. 615 and begin climbing this dirt and gravel road.

6.2 Turn left onto F.R. 90.

8.0 You will arrive back at the starting point.

Rail Trails

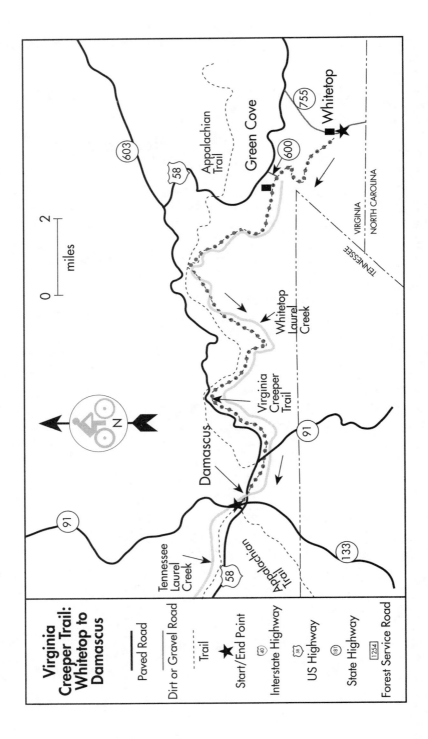

Virginia
Creeper Trail:
Whitetop to
Damascus

Paved Road

Dirt or Gravel Road

Trail

★ Start/End Point

Interstate Highway

US Highway

State Highway

Forest Service Road

Virginia Creeper Trail: Whitetop to Damascus

Distance: 17.5 miles

Difficulty: Easy to moderate

Riding surface: Original ballast path

Maps: 1. Mount Rogers National Recreation Area
2. USGS 7.5 minute quadrangle, Grayson, Tenn.-N.C.-Va.
3. USGS 7.5 minute quadrangle, Konnarock, Va.
4. USGS 7.5 minute quadrangle, Damascus, Va.
5. Guide to the Virginia Creeper Trail, available from Virginia Creeper Trail Club, P.O. Box 2382, Abingdon, Va. 24210

Access: To reach the Whitetop access, take U.S. 58 East from the intersection of U.S. 58 and Va. 91 near Damascus. Drive 9.5 miles to the intersection with Va. 603. Turn right to stay on U.S. 58. Drive 6.2 miles to the turnoff for Fire House Road (F.R. 755). Turn right onto Fire House Road and drive about 2 miles to the Whitetop parking area. Follow the signs to the Virginia Creeper Trail.

To reach the Green Cove access, follow the above directions to the intersection of U.S. 58 and Va. 603. Turn right to stay on U.S. 58, then drive 4.2 miles to the turnoff for Green Cove Road (F.R. 600). Turn right onto Green Cove Road and drive 0.3 mile to the Green Cove Station, on the right. Park here to begin.

To reach the Damascus access, take U.S. 58 West from the intersection of U.S. 58 and Va. 91. Drive through the town of Damascus for 1.5 miles to the red caboose at the Virginia Creeper trailhead, located on the left just across Tennessee Laurel Creek. Park in the parking area.

Note: U.S. 58 makes several turns through Damascus; just follow the highway signs and make the appropriate turns.

Elevation change: The ride begins at an elevation of 3,600 feet at Whitetop and drops to 3,200 feet at Green Cove, then all the way to 2,400 feet at Taylors Valley and 1,900 feet at Damascus. There is no elevation gain on this section, when ridden east to west. The total elevation *loss* is 1,700 feet.

Configuration: One-way

One of the 30 trestles or bridges that dot the Virginia Creeper Trail

O f the 14 rail trails I have pedaled in the Southeast, the Virginia Creeper Trail is my favorite. It stands head and shoulders above the rest, with the exception of the nearby New River Trail, which comes in a fairly close second. The Virginia Creeper Trail runs east to west for approximately 33 miles from the Whitetop Mountain area to Abingdon, through some of the highest and most scenic terrain known to any rail trail.

This crushed-stone pathway is the abandoned railway corridor of the old Virginia-Carolina Railroad, known in former days as the "V-C." The first steam locomotive huffed and puffed its way from Abingdon to Damascus back in February 1900. Later, this backwoods railroad line was lengthened all the way to Elkland, North Carolina. For many years, it was the only means of commercial transport from the high mountains to the valley towns of Abingdon and Damascus. Timber was hauled down from the mountains for processing in town, and occasionally, some of the mountain residents would hitch a ride on the train to and from the valley. These folks affectionately nicknamed the railroad "Virginia Creeper" for the slow crawl the locomotive made traveling west to east. Some people claim that the nickname also referred to the Virginia creeper vine growing near the tracks.

On March 31, 1977, the Virginia-Carolina Railroad made its last run. When the locomotive fell silent at the end of that historic day, some say the romance of the railroad era died. In the late 1950s, the Norfolk & Western Railroad Company presented the town of Abingdon with the old "V-C" steam locomotive for public display. It sits as a sentry at the trailhead in Abingdon and is a noble reminder of that period in American history.

Mile for mile, this trail is easy, though the distance can be taxing for some cyclists. If you set up a shuttle and ride east to west, you will pedal 17.5 easy miles. If you ride it as an out-and-back, the difficulty increases, due to the 1,700-foot elevation gain and the total distance of 35 miles. The surface of the trail consists of crushed rock and dirt and poses virtually no technical challenge. For the most part, it is well groomed, though you will find a few rocky stretches. Its gently descending grade, wide double track, smooth surface, and variety of ride options make the Virginia Creeper Trail an attractive mountain-bike ride for cyclists of diverse abilities.

The scenery on this eastern half of the trail is quite different from the section running from Damascus to Abingdon. The high-elevation hills play host to a variety of conifers not found at lower elevations. There is also a splash of high-elevation wildflowers, such as painted trillium, growing along this upper stretch of trail. During late spring and early summer, you can enjoy the dramatic show of rhododendron blossoms in the many thickets seen from the Virginia Creeper Trail.

Several miles of this railway corridor plunge through Whitetop Laurel Gorge, leading cyclists past very old geological formations. Rock outcroppings dress the banks of Whitetop Laurel Creek to create exceptionally beautiful scenery. There are also dramatic views from some of the 30 trestles and bridges you will cross. Signs at these trestles ask that you get off your bike and walk across. Better take heed. Hitting a bad spot on a 30-foot-high bridge and sailing over the rails might put a damper on your afternoon.

Don't be deceived by the name Whitetop Laurel *Creek*, for this is nothing like the benign, trickling threads of water normally considered *creeks*. In some sections, car-sized boulders choke the creek, causing the cold waters to squeeze past in a roaring rush. Some of the rapids are class V challenges which even the most experienced whitewater paddlers opt to portage. Along other sections, tumbling rapids drop into placid pools. These shimmering creek pools are delicious temptations for parched mountain bikers during the sweaty dog days of summer.

0.0 After leaving a shuttle vehicle in Damascus, begin cycling west on the Creeper from the Whitetop access.

0.7 There is a Christmas-tree farm on the right.

2.6 A locked gate and a Christmas-tree farm are on the left.

3.0 You will cross Green Cove Road and pedal through the Green Cove access; you can begin the ride here to shorten the mileage a bit. An old train station is located here. There is a portable toilet behind the train station.

4.1 You will pedal across a dirt road.

5.3   You will come to a trestle. Dismount and walk across the trestle, then cross a road and pedal around a gate.

6.7   The Appalachian Trail crosses the trail, goes off to the right, and joins the Virginia Creeper Trail for a distance. Just past this intersection with the Appalachian Trail, you will approach a high, 550-foot-long trestle at a creek junction. Walk across the trestle. There is a sign showing the mileage to Taylors Valley (4 miles) and Damascus (10 miles).

7.1   The Appalachian Trail leaves the Creeper and disappears into the woods on the right. Double white blazes indicate a change in direction for the Appalachian Trail.

9.9   You will come to a tiny trestle crossing and a sign showing the mileage to Straight Branch (3 miles) and Damascus (7 miles). On the right is F.R. 49100; take the lower trail and not this dirt road. Some houses are located here.

Old trail station at Green Cove

Expect to see kayaks and canoes on the swift whitewater of Whitetop Laurel Creek.

10.1 The trail crosses the road. There is a sign indicating that a vending site is ahead.

10.2 You will pedal through someone's front yard and pass through a gate; be sure to close the gate behind you, as the landowner has requested.

10.4 You will come to a trestle. There is a dirt road on the right. Dismount and walk across the trestle.

10.7 You will cross a dirt road. William Lane Dunn Bridge is on the left.

10.8 A vending area is on the right. Pedal around the gate; the river will be on your left.

12.2 You will come to a washed-out area of trail.

12.9 The Straight Branch parking lot is on the right. Beech Grove Trail and the Appalachian Trail go off to the right.

15.1 You will cross an iron bridge.

16.0 The trail parallels U.S. 58 near the intersection with Va. 91.

16.1 You will pedal across Va. 91; exercise caution on this busy highway.

16.8 You will pedal across a paved road; U.S. 58 bends around to the right.

17.2 You will pedal across North Shady Avenue.

17.3 You will cross a large bridge.

17.5 You will arrive at the Damascus access and the red caboose.

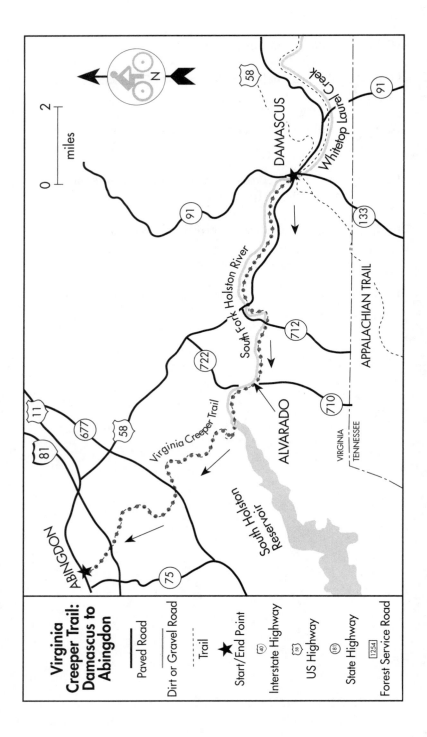

Virginia Creeper Trail: Damascus to Abingdon

Paved Road

Dirt or Gravel Road

Trail

★ Start/End Point

40 Interstate Highway

58 US Highway

18 State Highway

1254 Forest Service Road

DAMASCUS

ABINGDON

ALVARADO

Virginia Creeper Trail

South Fork Holston River

South Holston Reservoir

Whitetop Laurel Creek

APPALACHIAN TRAIL

VIRGINIA
TENNESSEE

N

miles
0   2

58

91

133

712

710

722

677

58

11

81

75

91

Virginia Creeper Trail: Damascus to Abingdon

Distance: 15 miles

Difficulty: Easy

Riding surface: Original ballast path

Maps: 1. Mount Rogers National Recreation Area
2. USGS 7.5 minute quadrangle, Damascus, Va.
3. USGS 7.5 minute quadrangle, Abingdon, Va.
4. Guide to the Virginia Creeper Trail, available from Virginia Creeper Trail Club, P.O. Box 2382, Abingdon, Va. 24210

Access: To reach the Damascus access, take U.S. 58 West from the intersection of U.S. 58 and Va. 91. Drive through the town of Damascus for 1.5 miles to the red caboose at the Virginia Creeper trailhead, located on the left just across Tennessee Laurel Creek. Park in the parking area.

Note: U.S. 58 makes several turns through Damascus; just follow the highway signs and make the appropriate turns.

To reach the Abingdon access, drive west on U.S. 58 into the town of Abingdon. Head through the quaint downtown area to a traffic light marked as Signal #3. You will see a sign for the Virginia Creeper Trail pointing left; turn left onto Pecan Street SE. The parking lot for the trailhead is on the right about 0.2 mile from Signal #3. The trail begins across the street. An old locomotive is on display at the trailhead.

Elevation change: The elevation at Damascus is about 1,900 feet. You will pedal a slight descent for a few miles to a minimum of 1,750 feet at the South Fork of the Holston River. The elevation then rises to about 2,050 feet by the end of the trail in Abingdon. The total elevation gain is about 300 feet.

Configuration: One-way

The old Virginia-Carolina locomotive sits at the Abingdon trailhead.

Hundreds of years ago, the tracks along this pathway were mostly those of plodding buffalo and those of moccasin-clad Indians silently slipping from the valleys into the high mountains to hunt. Later came the rugged boots of early colonial frontiersmen, including Daniel Boone.

With the arrival of the 20th century, new tracks appeared in this swath of southwest Virginia. But these tracks were long and silver and belonged to a hissing, clanking beast, the steam locomotive. "Civilization" had finally arrived in the mountains, on the shoulders of the Virginia-Carolina Railroad.

Today, the railway has been abandoned and the rails and crossties removed, leaving only a smooth, wide path rambling through the Virginia hills. But fresh tracks have emerged, thanks to local efforts and a lot of hard work. There are the boot tracks of hikers, not colonial pioneers. There are the tracks of horses belonging to insurance salesmen and dentists, not early frontiersmen. And there is a new kind of track unique to our time: the waffle prints of mountain-bike tires.

Like its eastern mate, this half of the Virginia Creeper Trail is nontechnical and has a well-groomed surface of crushed stone. It is also an easy trail if pedaled as a one-way shuttle ride. However, if ridden as an out-and-back, this western section of the Creeper is a good bit easier than the eastern section. Its round-trip elevation gain is only 450 feet, which is quite a contrast to the 1,700 feet gained from Damascus to Whitetop.

The scenery on the western section is also remarkably different from the eastern leg. Rather than running beside cascading white water, this section hugs the banks of the slowly flowing South Fork of the Holston River. You will cross 13 bridges and trestles, some over the river and others over deep, junglelike ravines.

The trail doesn't slice through any rocky gorges between Damascus and Abingdon, but it does flow past beautiful, rolling pastureland that will have you pedaling quite close to grazing horses and cattle. My group even pedaled through one pasture filled only with bulls. Though it was unnerving for a moment, we were comforted by the fact that the bulls didn't seem a bit interested in mountain bikers. However, I was glad that I'd left my very *red* windbreaker on the back seat of my car.

Along the trail, there are 10 private gates you will have to stop, open, and pass through. Be sure to close them behind you so the animals will stay home where they belong.

0.0   Pedal across U.S. 58 away from the caboose.

1.3   You will pedal across a paved road.

2.9   You will pedal across another paved road.

3.4   You will pedal beneath a bridge and pass through a metal gate; be sure to close the gate behind you.

You'll see cattle, bulls, horses—and maybe even baby donkeys—along this trail.

4.9   You will pedal across a road. A metal bridge is on the right.

6.7   The trail crosses a road in the town of Alvarado. Alvarado Bible Church is on your left.

7.9   You will pedal through a gate, then across a long, high bridge above South Holston Lake.

9.3   You will pedal through a gate and cross a long bridge. Don't forget to dismount and walk across the bridge.

9.5   You will cross a road and then pass through a gate. Be sure to close the gate behind you.

10.4   You will cross a very high bridge. Don't look down!

11.3   You will cycle to the left of a permanent iron gate.

11.4   You will cross a paved road.

13.7 You will come to a golf-cart crossing and pedal past Glenrochie Country Club.

14.0 You will pedal under I-81.

15.0 You will reach the end of the trail in Abingdon.

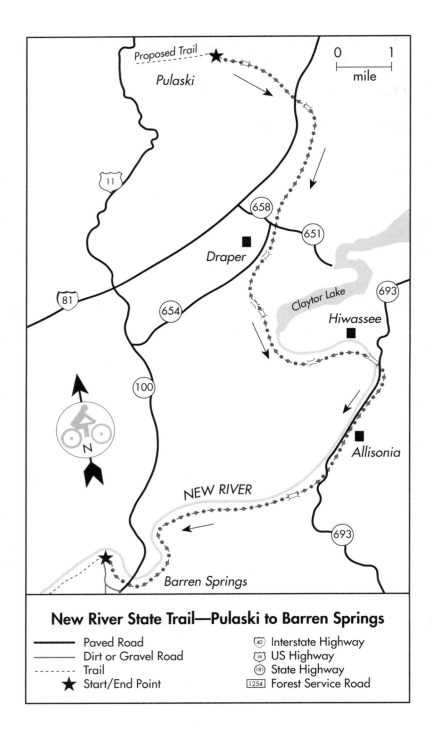

Proposed Trail

Pulaski

11

658

651

Draper

693

81

654

Claytor Lake

Hiwassee

100

Allisonia

NEW RIVER

N

693

Barren Springs

New River State Trail—Pulaski to Barren Springs

Paved Road

Dirt or Gravel Road

Trail

★ Start/End Point

⓸ Interstate Highway

⑤⑧ US Highway

⑱ State Highway

1254 Forest Service Road

0 1
mile

New River Trail:
Pulaski to Barren Springs

Distance: 15.4 miles

Difficulty: Easy to moderate

Riding surface: Original ballast path

Maps: 1. New River Trail State Park Trail Guide,
available from New River Trail State Park,
Route 1, Box 81X, Austinville, Va. 24312
(703-699-6778)
2. New River Trail State Park, available from
Custom CAD Maps, Route 1, Box 117-A1,
Draper, Va. 24324

Access: To reach the Pulaski access, take Exit 94 off I-81
and drive north on Va. 99 for 1.8 miles. Turn right onto
Xaloy Way at the brown sign for New River Trail State
Park's northern terminus. The parking area for the trail is
on the right less than 0.1 mile from the turnoff.

To reach the Barren Springs access, take the U.S. 100
exit off I-81. Drive south on U.S. 100. You will cross the
New River after 5.9 miles. Continue another 0.3 mile, then
turn right onto Lone Ash Road (F.R. 622). Turn right onto
F.R. 620 almost immediately. Drive 0.4 mile through a community of houses to a parking area near the trail. This is
not an officially developed access to the trail, but
there is an area where half a dozen or so vehicles can park.

Note: Barren Springs was recommended to me by the
park service as the southernmost access (above Shot Tower)
for entering or leaving the trail. The trail does extend

southward from Barren Springs to Shot Tower, but there is a 2-mile section that is currently closed to the public due to a landowner dispute. You can pedal south of Barren Springs up to the trail-closure signs, but there is no public parking area.

There are additional access points north of Shot Tower. The only other developed access point is located at Draper. Undeveloped access points are located at Hiwassee and Allisonia.

Elevation change: The elevation at Pulaski is 1,900 feet. The ride climbs to 2,100 feet in the first 3 miles and then steadily drops for the next 7 miles until it reaches 1,850 feet. The rest of the ride is on a mostly level grade. The final elevation is 1,900 feet at Barren Springs. The total elevation gain is 250 feet.

If you ride this as an out-and-back from Pulaski, the greatest climb is on the return ride on a 2-mile stretch near Draper. The elevation climbs from 1,850 feet to 2,100 feet in this section.

Configuration: One-way

Expansive views of the New River are best appreciated from the bridges.

Swinging around a bend in the trail, I gently squeezed my brake levers and came to a slow stop. I listened. As I stood there with my bike against my leg, the only sounds I heard were my own breathing and a few melodic trills from nearby birds. Looking down at the wide path stretching before me, I could only imagine what sounds were made on this very spot back in the late 1800s. It wasn't the high-pitched sound of spinning bicycle tires, it wasn't the clip-clop of horses' hooves, and it certainly wasn't the crunch of hiking boots on crushed stones. No, the most common sounds along this path were probably the wail of train whistles and the hiss of steam locomotives as they chugged along the steel rails once embedded in this track.

These beautiful miles of trail threading through the rolling green hills of southwest Virginia were once part of the railroad right of way used by the Norfolk & Western Railroad Company. Lead, iron, copper, and other minerals were in rich supply in this part of the country. As a result, mining flourished here, and many manufacturing companies sprang up. The railroad was constructed to service this thriving industry, transporting the mining spoils from the hills of Virginia to the rest of America. People looking for work moved into the area, and towns were born along the rail line, many of which are still in existence today. Though the times were tough and the days long and hard, the mining business of southwest Virginia prospered.

Today, the locomotives are history and the old crossties have been removed, leaving only the memories of a bygone era. This abandoned railway corridor is one of America's popular rail trails, part of a recent movement to utilize old railroad rights of way as parks for public recreation. New River Trail is Virginia's only linear park, or greenway. It is a multiuse trail, with nearly all of its 57 miles now open to the public. The result is a happy mingling of bicyclists, hikers, and equestrians. Most of the trail work was done by volunteers, so if you run into one, be sure to give him or her a grateful pat on the back.

The trail is not technically challenging, but you *will* need a mountain bike or, at the very least, an all-terrain bicycle. Forget the skinny-tired bikes that work so well on pavement. You

Expect to pass some horses on the New River Trail.

will need fat, knobby tires for the loose gravel and for rolling over rocks.

You will sometimes coast or pedal easily through splendid Virginia hill country. Rolling farmland dotted with cattle, beautiful green hills, and wildflower-filled meadows will envelop you along some sections. Other sections offer a striking contrast, with sheer rock walls soaring high above the trail on one side and the shimmering water of the New River placidly drifting by on the other. Tall grasses bend in the gentle breezes, and handfuls of brightly colored wildflowers push up through the moist soil to drink in the mild sunshine. On a spring ride, I noticed patches of sweet white violets growing in cracks in the rock walls. Set against the rugged sharpness of the cold stones, these flowers looked like the most delicate, fragile things on earth. It was a stunning juxtaposition of young, fleeting flowers set against old, eternal rock.

Twenty-nine miles of the New River Trail hug the banks of the river, creating an especially scenic mountain-bike ride. Not only will you pedal beside this, the second-oldest river in the world, but you will also pedal over it. In the northern section of the trail, there are eight bridges and trestles, some of which offer incredibly expansive views. One bridge is especially memorable, due to its precarious height above the river. If you have a fear of heights, you'll be in therapy after crossing this bridge. If you don't have a fear of heights, you will soon. As spooked as I felt crossing this bridge with a 25-pound bicycle, I could only imagine how the old engineers felt rattling across in trains weighing hundreds of thousands of pounds.

0.0   The ride begins from the Pulaski parking area.

0.4   You will pedal across a wooden trestle over Peak Creek.

1.6   You will pass under I-81.

1.8   You will pedal across a wooden trestle over a road.

4.0   You will pedal across S.R. 651 in Draper. New River Bicycles is located nearby; here, you can arrange some bike repairs or buy parts, accessories, and snacks.

4.2   You will pedal past the Draper access parking lot. A portable toilet and a convenience store are located near this access point.

4.6   You will pedal across a long wooden trestle over a small creek.

4.8   You will pedal across a gravel drive about 20 feet from a paved road.

5.7   You will pedal across a wooden trestle over a narrow, paved road.

6.0   You will pedal across the highest wooden trestle on the trail.

7.0 You will pedal across a wooden trestle; some homes are on the right.

8.2 You will pedal across a major bridge over the New River at Hiwassee; this bridge is 951 feet long.

8.4 You will pedal across S.R. 693 in Hiwassee.

9.2 You will pedal across a dirt road.

10.3 You will pedal through the small community of Allisonia. Allisonia United Methodist Church, built in 1891, is located here.

10.4 You will pedal across a paved road.

11.1 You will pedal across a bridge over the New River. Near this site is the river-level gauging station. Years ago, the gauging station operator would climb into a cable car and scoot along a cable strung across the river. At the center of the river, he would lower a weighted measuring cord into the water to obtain the river's depth.

11.8 A waterfall is on the left.

14.3 A huge, chimneylike rock structure is on the left side of the trail.

15.2 You will pedal under the U.S. 100 bridge.

15.4 You will arrive at the Barren Springs access and the parking area.

Note: If you would like to arrange shuttle service, bike rentals, or other trail-related services at the Draper access, contact Lanny Sparks, New River Bicycles, Ltd., Route 1, Box 175, Draper, Va. 24324 (703-980-1741). If you would like to arrange trail-related services at the Barren Springs access, contact Dennis Barnes, Denny's Stop & Go, Routes 698 and 100, Barren Springs, Va. 24324 (703-766-3206). Dennis Barnes advertises "Guaranteed Friendly Service," and, for a change, you'll find truth in advertising.

Long, sturdy bridges highlight the ride.

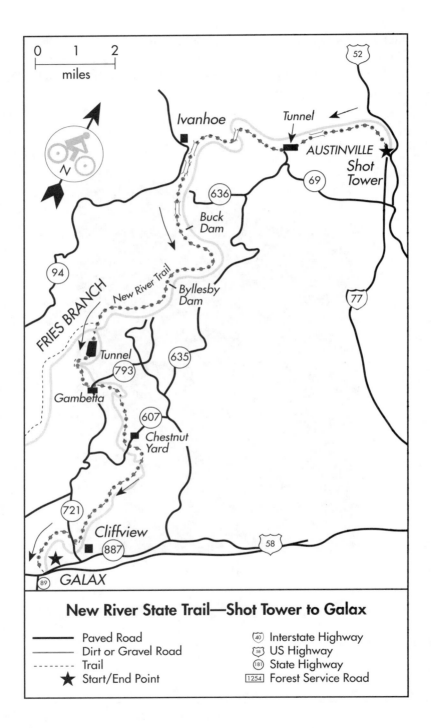

0　　1　　2
miles

Ivanhoe

Tunnel

Tunnel

AUSTINVILLE

Shot Tower

(52)

(636)

Buck Dam

(69)

(94)

New River Trail

FRIES BRANCH

Byllesby Dam

(77)

Tunnel

(793)

(635)

Gambetta

(607)

Chestnut Yard

(721)

Cliffview

(887)

(58)

(89) **GALAX**

New River State Trail—Shot Tower to Galax

—— Paved Road	(40) Interstate Highway
—— Dirt or Gravel Road	(58) US Highway
---- Trail	(18) State Highway
★ Start/End Point	1254 Forest Service Road

New River Trail: Shot Tower to Galax

Distance: 26.1 miles

Difficulty: Easy to moderate

Riding surface: Original ballast path

Maps: 1. New River Trail State Park Trail Guide,
available from New River Trail State Park,
Route 1, Box 81X, Austinville, Va. 24312
(703-699-6778)
2. New River Trail State Park, available from
Custom CAD Maps, Route 1, Box 117-A1,
Draper, Va. 24324

Access: To reach the Shot Tower access, take Exit 24 off
I-77 and head east on Va. 69. Drive 0.3 mile to a stop sign.
Turn left onto U.S. 52 North, following the signs for Shot
Tower Historical Park and New River Trail Park. After 1.4
miles, turn left at a sign for Shot Tower. This road looks
like a driveway to a farmhouse. You will pass by white picket
fences, nice farm homes, and big barns. Park in the parking area designated for the New River Trail, which is adja-
cent to the Shot Tower Historical Park drive.

To reach the Galax access, take Exit 14 off I-77. Drive
west on U.S. 58 for 10 miles; you will pass through the
town of Galax. The parking area for the trail is well marked.
It is located on the right just past Chestnut Creek.

Note: There are additional access points south of Shot
Tower. The other developed access points are located at
Buck Dam, Byllesby Dam, Gambetta, Chestnut Yard, and
Cliffview. There are horse- and bike-rental outfits in
Cliffview. Undeveloped access points are located at

Austinville and Ivanhoe. All of these access points were train stops during railroad days.

Elevation change: The elevation at Shot Tower is 1,950 feet. The ride gradually climbs over the next 25 miles to a maximum 2,350 feet. The total elevation gain is 400 feet. Riding this trail in the opposite direction—from south to north, or from Galax to Shot Tower—is an even easier route, with an elevation *loss* of 400 feet.

Configuration: One-way

Back in 1807, Englishman Thomas Jackson probably never dreamed that the shot tower he built would be designated a National Historic Mechanical Engineering Landmark almost 200 years later. This 75-foot-high stone tower was built on a bluff, with a 75-foot-deep shaft below the structure. Crude wooden stairs led up to the top level, which contained a fireplace and a chimney. It was here that slaves placed lead in a kettle, melted it, and then poured it through sieves. The molten lead fell 150 feet from the top of the tower to a kettle of water waiting on the floor of the shaft. This distance of 150 feet supposedly ensured the uniform roundness of the shot. The shot was later retrieved from the kettle through an access tunnel that connected the New River and the shaft. Quite a few critters were served up for supper with the aid of the shot made in Jackson's now-famous tower.

Today, Shot Tower stands as a testament to the enterprise and industry of a fledgling, yet quickly growing, America. It also serves as the midway point of New River Trail State Park, and as its headquarters. It provides a good starting point for many of the ride options offered by this 57-mile-long abandoned railroad right of way.

The historical highlights along this rail trail are not concentrated simply around Shot Tower. One of the first points of interest you will reach as you pedal south toward Galax is the town of Austinville. General Andrew Lewis, Daniel Boone, and many other colonial frontiersmen reportedly stopped at

Shot Tower

Austinville, known then as the "Lead Mines." It was in this small mining town that the Fincastle Resolutions, a precursor of the Declaration of Independence, were written.

The mining of lead was a thriving industry that began in the late 1700s. Austinville was the site of a number of mines. At the time of the Civil War, the mines were incorporated and consolidated as the Wythe Union Lead Mine Company. Its name notwithstanding, the company was the chief supplier of lead to the Confederate troops. The name didn't fool the Yankees, as the company was attacked twice during the war.

Before you pedal away from Austinville, you might want to stop by the Austin Homestead, the home of Moses Austin, who gave the town its name. This man owned the local lead mines and was the father of Stephen F. Austin, the "Father of Texas." It is believed that Stephen Austin was born in this old house near the slowly rolling waters of the New River.

Just like the northern half of the New River Trail, this ride is relatively easy. There are no screaming descents, no challenging climbs, and no technical single-track sections that dangle you from 1,000-foot cliffs. What you will find as you spin down the trail is a peaceful ride set in exceptionally beautiful backwoods country. The trail is wide and has a nontechnical surface of crushed rock. You might even see some cinders on this old railroad bed, leftovers from the coal burned to power the steam locomotives. Most sections are smooth and well groomed, though there are a few bumpy areas where horse hooves have made deep indentations in the soft soil.

This 26-mile trail offers excellent opportunities for overnight bike camping. Water is plentiful, and there are many inviting spots along the river to set up camp. The terrain is easy enough that most cyclists can handle the additional weight of gear-filled panniers. As you pedal along, you will see why this trail seems ideal for overnight guests on two wheels.

Most of the trail parrots the moves of the New River and Chestnut Creek, slowly winding through the gaps and saddles of the mountains. In some sections, you will pedal next to calm, clear water that seems to barely flow. In other sections, the pulse of the river quickens to frothy, thundering rapids. You will cross the river and creek a lucky 13 times on the southern half of the trail via sturdy bridges and restored trestles. Some are short and hover only a few feet above the water, while others are long and high. Though these bridges might give some folks heart palpitations, the vistas offered from their heights are truly stunning.

If all of this isn't enough, how does pedaling blindly through a dark, damp stone tunnel grab you? The trail disappears into two tunnels, one of which is particularly memorable as it curves for 229 feet through cold, wet, pitch-dark blackness. As you approach this tunnel, try to imagine its construction back in the late 1800s. Workmen had the benefit of only crude tools and dynamite to barrel a path through the mountain. Makes me exhausted just to think of the work involved. The temperature inside the tunnel is dramatically cooler than outside. Most of the time, icy droplets of water drip from crevices in the stone. Pedaling past the mouth of the tunnel and into the dark cavern, you might experience for a moment what Jonah must have felt in the belly of the great fish. But in no time, the tunnel spits you back into a sun-drenched world that will have you squinting as your eyes try to adjust to the light.

As you move down the trail, you will spin through a beautiful forest of mixed hardwoods, pines, hemlocks, and rhododendron. In the spring, you will pedal deep into a world of pastel colors, as blooming dogwoods brighten the high ridges and wildflowers dot the newly green riverbanks like pale yellow and lavender Easter eggs. Summertime rides are generally comfortable, due to the canopy of shade offered by mature oaks and other hardwoods. This same deciduous forest promises a vibrant show of color in autumn, when the hills of Virginia seem to catch on fire.

0.0   From the parking area next to Shot Tower Historical Park, turn left and pedal down the road.

0.2   Turn left onto a climbing dirt path that leads to the river. The U.S. 52 bridge is on your right. This bridge replaced Jackson's Ferry, a hand-drawn ferry owned and operated by Thomas Jackson and his descendants from 1758 to 1930.

0.4   Shot Tower Loop Trail is on the left. Pedal under I-77.

2.7   You will pedal across a wooden trestle.

2.8   A shelter and picnic table are on the left.

Buck Dam

The longer of the two tunnels on the New River Trail State Park.

3.3 You will cycle through a 193-foot tunnel.

3.7 You will pedal across a busy street. Exercise caution.

4.2 The trail skirts the James River Limestone Company, an abandoned industrial area. Warning signs advise trail users not to stray from the trail, due to the hazardous nature of this industrial area.

5.2 You will pedal across a wooden trestle.

6.5 The Ivanhoe parking lot is on the right. You will notice a large, rusted object in the center of this large parking area. One of the park rangers told me that it's a stone crusher.

6.6 You will pedal across a 670-foot wooden trestle.

7.2 You will pedal across a wooden trestle.

7.8 You will pedal across a road.

8.0 You will pedal through a community of houses.

8.8 You will pedal across a wooden trestle.

9.4 A portable toilet is on the left; a picnic table and shelter are on the right.

9.6 The impressive-looking Buck Dam is on the left. You will pedal across a dirt road.

10.4 Ruth's Spring is on the right, along with a trail shelter.

10.9 You will pedal across a road.

11.9 Byllesby Dam is on the left. You will pedal across Byllesby Road (F.R. 602). The Appalachian Power Byllesby Hydroelectric Company is on the right.

12.7 A trail shelter and picnic table are on your right.

14.0 You will pedal across a wooden trestle. A portable toilet and picnic tables are on the right.

14.5 Fries Branch Trail leaves the main trail and branches off to the right. Picnic tables and a shelter are located at this trail junction. Stay on the main trail. You will pedal across a very long bridge over the New River. Chestnut Creek merges into the New River at this point.

15.3 You will pedal through a 229-foot tunnel, the longer of the two tunnels on the trail. Chestnut Creek is on your left.

16.9 You will cross a road. Just past the road, you will pedal across a wooden trestle over Chestnut Creek.

18.0 You will pedal across a wooden trestle over the creek.

19.9 You will cross a road; a shelter is located here.

20.6 You will pedal across a short wooden trestle.

20.9 You will pedal across a bridge. Chestnut Creek Waterfall, also known as Six Pack Waterfall, is on the left. A shelter is on the northern side of the bridge.

23.9 You will pedal across a busy street. The Cliffview Trading Post is located at this crossing. Stables and a horse-rental facility are located next to the store. On the right is the parking area for the Cliffview access.

25.5 You will pedal across a wooden trestle.

25.6 You will cross a road and then a wooden trestle over Chestnut Creek.

26.1 You will reach the southern terminus of the New River Trail at the Galax access.

Note: There are many different ways to cycle this half of the New River Trail. The easiest way to pedal these 26 miles is to leave a vehicle at the Shot Tower parking area and begin riding in Galax. It's all downhill.

If you want to pedal this half of the trail as an out-and-back ride, you will probably want to begin at Shot Tower so that you can get the (easy) climbing out of the way in the first half of the ride. The total distance is then a little over 52 miles.

Stone crusher at Ivanhoe

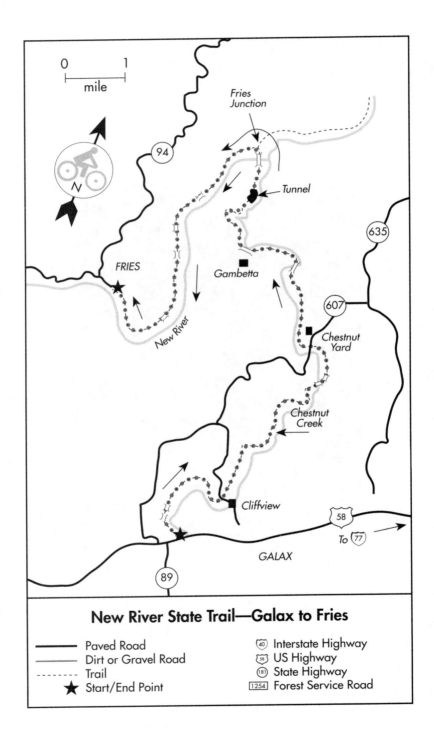

0
1
mile

94

Fries
Junction

Tunnel

635

FRIES

Gambetta

607

Chestnut
Yard

Chestnut
Creek

New River

Cliffview

58

To 77

GALAX

89

New River State Trail—Galax to Fries

———— Paved Road	ⓐ Interstate Highway
———— Dirt or Gravel Road	ⓢ US Highway
- - - - Trail	ⓢ State Highway
★ Start/End Point	1254 Forest Service Road

New River Trail: Galax to Fries

Distance: 16.9 miles

Difficulty: Easy to moderate

Riding surface: Original ballast path

Maps: 1. New River Trail State Park Trail Guide, available from New River Trail State Park, Route 1, Box 81X, Austinville, Va. 24312 (703-699-6778)
2. New River Trail State Park, available from Custom CAD Maps, Route 1, Box 117-A1, Draper, Va. 24324

Access: To reach the Galax access, take Exit 14 off I-77. Drive west on U.S. 58 for 10 miles; you will pass through the town of Galax. The parking area for the trail is well marked. It is located on the right just past Chestnut Creek.

To reach the Fries Branch access, begin at the intersection of U.S. 58/U.S. 221 and N.C. 94 and follow N.C. 94 for approximately 4.5 miles to the town of Fries (pronounced freeze). The parking area for the New River Trail is located on Main Street between Riverview Avenue and Anderson Drive.

Note: There are additional access points in this section. The other developed access points are at Cliffview, Chestnut Yard, and Gambetta. All of these were former train stops during railroad days.

Elevation change: The ride begins at an elevation of 2,350 feet in Galax and drops to 2,100 feet at the Fries Branch junction. It then climbs to 2,150 feet at the Fries terminus. The total elevation gain on this one-way stretch is only 50 feet, but if you make this an out-and-back ride from Galax to Fries to Galax, the total elevation gain is 300 feet.

Configuration: One-way

The trail closely parallels the New River.

The beauty of a rail trail like the New River Trail is its appeal to almost any type of bicyclist. You don't have to be an expert mountain-bike racer to fully appreciate all this trail has to offer. Any cyclist—including beginners, children, senior citizens, and occasional cyclists—will find this trail easy when pedaled in part. And because of its impressive one-way length, stronger cyclists also enjoy the New River Trail. Many experienced riders find that it offers an appealing change of pace from the rough-and-tumble world of challenging single track. The trail also offers a long, steady workout unbroken by traffic and trail obstacles.

This trail is actually an abandoned rail corridor once used by the Norfolk & Western Railroad Company. The right of way was donated to the state of Virginia for use as a park and has now been restored to become the state's first linear park. Fifty-seven miles of trail stretch from Pulaski to Galax, with a short southwestern leg branching off to the town of Fries. Most of the 57 miles are open to the public and are heavily used by cyclists, hikers, joggers, horseback riders, and even cross-country skiers.

This particular ride from Galax to Fries follows a wide double-track trail with a smooth crushed-rock surface. Horses have created some rutted areas in a few sections, though these bumpy spots can be easily negotiated. You might expect to find crowds of trail users on this popular path, but the long length tends to spread folks out. The closer you are to a major access point, though, the greater the number of people you will pass.

As you pedal, you will be flanked by beautiful pastoral scenery. The trail meanders past rolling green farmland and visits grazing cattle, who occasionally lift their heads to study passing cyclists. For almost its entire 17 miles, the trail parallels the sparkling waters of Chestnut Creek and the New River. Because of the slow-moving water in most sections of the New River, this is a popular destination for canoeists wishing to pole, rather than paddle, their way through its shallow waters.

A fatal train wreck occurred in 1928 near the junction of the New River and Chestnut Creek. A passenger train backing into Fries was struck by a freight train leaving town nearly 30 minutes behind schedule. Apparently, the freight train was traveling so fast that it split the end coach of the passenger train completely in half. It is said that the wooden car burst apart like a split melon, leaving the two sides lying on opposite sides of the track.

0.0 Begin cycling from the Galax parking area.

0.5 You will cross a wooden trestle over Chestnut Creek and then pedal across a road.

0.6 You will pedal across a wooden trestle.

2.2 The Cliffview access is on the left. You will pedal across a busy street. A convenience store and facilities for horse and bicycle rental are located at this trail access.

5.2 You will pedal across a bridge; there is a waterfall on the right. Just past the bridge is a trail shelter.

5.5 You will pedal across a short wooden trestle.

6.2 You will cross a road; a shelter is located here.

8.1 You will pedal across a wooden trestle over the creek.

9.2 You will pedal across a wooden trestle over Chestnut Creek. Just past this trestle, you will cross a road.

10.8 You will pedal through a 229-foot tunnel.

11.6 You will pedal across a long bridge over the New River. Chestnut Creek merges into the New River at this point. Turn left onto the Fries Branch.

12.3 You will pedal across a wooden trestle.

13.1 You will pedal across another wooden trestle.

13.7 You will cross another wooden trestle.

14.3 You will cross yet another wooden trestle.

15.0 You will cross a road. A convenience store is located at this intersection.

15.2 You will pedal across a wooden trestle.

15.9 You will cross a dirt road.

16.6 You will pedal across a wooden trestle.

16.9 You will arrive at the Fries Branch access.

Horses can be rented at the Cliffview Access.

Index